All About Birds

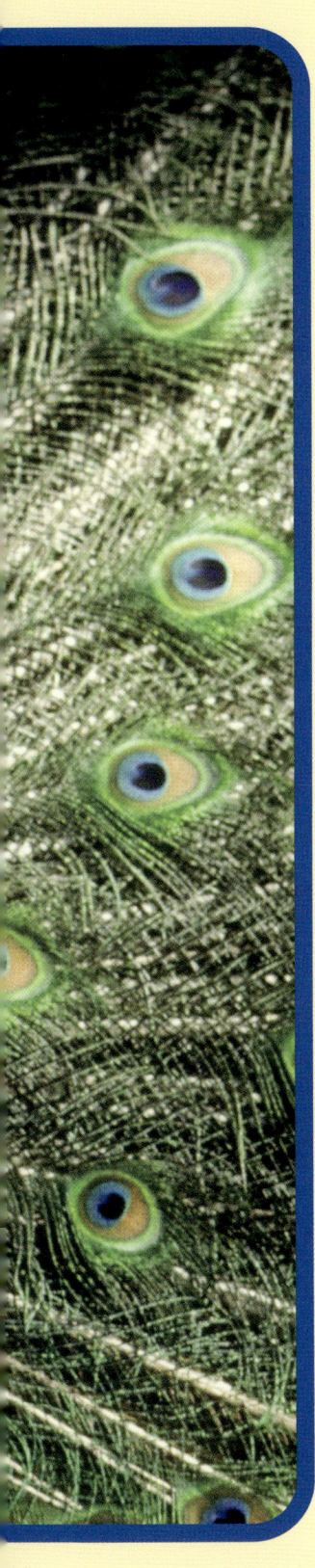

All About Birds

A Supplement to
Childcraft—The How and Why Library

World Book, Inc.
a Scott Fetzer company
Chicago

For information about other World Book publications, visit our Web site http://www.worldbook.com or call **1-800-WORLDBK (967-5325).** For information about sales to schools and libraries, call **1-800-975-3250 (United States); 1-800-837-5365 (Canada).**

"There Once Was a Puffin" by Florence Page Jaques. By permission of the University of Minnesota Press.

World Book, Inc.
233 N. Michigan Ave.
Chicago, IL 60601 U.S.A.

Printed in the United States of America

1 2 3 4 5 6 7 8 10 09 08 07 06 05

Library of Congress Cataloging-in-Publication Data

All about birds: a supplement to Childcraft--The How and Why
   Library.
     p. cm.
   "Revised and retitled edition of: Feathered friends, the 1983
Childcraft annual."
   Includes bibliographical references and index.
   ISBN 0-7166-0613-5
   1. Birds—Juvenile literature. I. World Book, Inc. II. Feathered
friends. III. Childcraft--the how and why library. Supplement.
QL676.3.A36 2005
598--dc22

2005005808

Staff

Editor in Chief
Paul A. Kobasa

Executive Editor
Sara Dreyfuss

Editorial

Managing Editor, General Publishing and Annuals
Maureen Mostyn Liebenson

Editor
Christine Sullivan

Assistant Editor
Lisa Kwon

Permissions Editor
Janet T. Peterson

Indexer
David Pofelski, *Head*
Aamir Burki

Writers
Karen Ingebretsen
Mary Kayaian
Sheri Reda

Graphics and Design

Manager
Sandra Dyrlund

Designers
Kim Saar
Don DiSante

Photographs Editors
Sylvia Ohlrich
Carol Parden

Production and Administrative Assistant
John Whitney

Research

Manager, Research Services
Loranne Shields

Researchers
Michael Barr
Cheryl Graham

Librarian
Jon Fjortoft

Product Production

Director, Manufacturing and Pre-press
Carma Fazio

Senior Production Manager
Madelyn Underwood

Production Manager
Anne Fritzinger

Manufacturing Manager
Barbara Podczerwinski

Text Processing
Curley Hunter
Gwendolyn Johnson

Proofreader
Anne Dillon

Marketing

Director, Direct Marketing
Mark Willy

Marketing Analyst
Zofia Kulik

Adviser

Mary Hennen
Collections Assistant—Bird Division
The Field Museum
Chicago, Illinois

Contents

Credits

The publishers of *Childcraft* gratefully acknowledge the sources listed below for the photographs in this volume. The publishers also acknowledge the following artists and agencies for their illustrations in this volume: Peter Babakitis, John F. Eggert, John Fleck, Albert E. Gilbert, Jean Helmer, Richard Hook, Pamela Ford Johnson, Walter Linsenmaier, Harry McNaugnt, Athos Menaloni, Yoshi Miyake, Oxford Illustrators Inc., Heidi Palmer, Roberta Polfus, Q2A, John Rignall, John Sanford, Arthur Singer, Samantha Carol Smith, Nancy Lee Walter, and Patricia Wynne. The credits shown below should be read from left to right, top to bottom, on their respective pages. All illustrations are the exclusive property of the publishers of *Childcraft*.

Covers:
Aristocrat, Discovery, International and Standard Bindings:
John Sanford
Heritage Binding:
©Craig K. Lorenz, Photo Researchers; Richard Hook; ©Eric & David Hosking, Corbis; Yoshi Miyake; ©Peter Oxford, Nature Picture Library; Yoshi Miyake; ©Kevin Schafer, Corbis; Patricia Wayne; ©Joe McDonald, Corbis
Rainbow Binding:
©Frans Lantig, Minden Pictures

2-3 © Ron Watts, Corbis

8-9 © Ron Austig; © David Hosking, Photo Researchers

16-17 © Gordon & Cathy Illg, AnimalsAnimals; © Roy Morsch, Corbis

18-19 © Patrico Robles Gil, Nature Picture Library

20-21 © Joe McDonald, Corbis

26-27 © C.C. Lockwood, AnimalsAnimals; © D. Robert & Lorri Franz, Corbis

28-29 © Kevin Fleming, Corbis; © David Welling, AnimalsAnimals

38-33 © Len Rue, Jr., AnimalsAnimals; © Konrad Wothe, Minden Pictures

40-41 © KonradArgus, Peter Arnold, Inc.

46-47 © Konrad Darrell Gulin, Corbis; © Roger Tidman, Corbis

56-57 © KonradMitsuaki Iwago, Minden Pictures; © Konrad Peter Johnson, Corbis

58-59 © Konrad Joe McDonald, Corbis; © Konrad Craig K. Lorenz, Photo Researchers

64-65 © Klaus Nigge/Foto Natura, Minden Pictures; ©Eric & David Hosking, Corbis

68-69 © Carol Hughes

70-71 © Wally McNamee, Corbis; © Joe McDonald, Corbis

78-79 © Henry R. Fox, AnimalsAnimals

82-83 © Michael S. Yamshita, Corbis; © Jeff Vanuga, Corbis

84-85 © Frans Lanting, Minden Pictures; Nancy Lee Walter

88-89 © Jen & Des Barlett, Bruce Coleman Inc.

90-91 © Wayne Lankinen, Bruce Coleman Inc.;

94-95 © Colin Varndell, Bruce Coleman Inc.; © Darrell Gulin, Corbis

100-101 © Kevin Schafer, Corbis

102-103 © Eric & David Hosking, Corbis

104-105 © Eric Soder, Photo Researchers; © Craig K. Lorenz, Photo Researchers

111 © Scott Nielson, Bruce Coleman Inc.

114-115 © Ron Sanford, Corbis; © John A.L. Cooke, AnimalsAnimals

120-121 © Corbis

122-123 © Gerry Ellis, Minden Pictures

126-127 © Eric & David Hosking. Corbis

130-131 © Peter Oxford, Nature Picture Library; © John Cancalosi, Bruce Coleman Collection

136-137 © Michael & Patricia Fogden, Minden Pictures; © J. Furman, Vireo

142-143 © Eric Crichton, Bruce Coleman Inc.; © Phil Savoie, Nature Picture Library

148-149 © John Storjohann, St. Louis Zoo

150-151 © James Hancock, Nature Photograhers, Ltd.; © Gerald Lacz, AnimalsAnimals

154-155 © Paul & Joyce Berquist, AnimalsAnimals; ©Noella Ballenger, Alamy

160-161 © Peter Johnson, Corbis; © John Cancalosi, Bruce Coleman Collection

164-165 © Craig K. Lorenz, Photo Researchers

168-169 © Hubert Stadler, Corbis; © Corbis

177 © Tui De Roy, Bruce Coleman Inc.

178-179 © Bruce M. Wellman, Tom Stack & Associates

184-185 © M.P.Harris, Bruce Coleman Inc.

186-187 © Fritz Polking/Frank Lane Picture Agency, Corbis

188-189 © Bryan & Cherry Alexander, Photo Researchers

192-193 © Bryan & Cherry Alexander Photography

198-199 © Daniel J. Cox, Corbis; © Arthur Morris, Corbis

200-201 ©Mike Wilkes, Nature Picture Library

Preface

Whether you live at the edge of a desert or in the middle of a crowded city, you probably see some birds every day. In fact, there are more than 9,000 different kinds of birds. But most of us do not pay much attention to them and do not know much about them. That's too bad, because birds are really marvelous creatures. They do many interesting—and sometimes amazing—things.

Birds are also very important to the balance of nature. By eating insects, many birds help keep insects from becoming too numerous. And some kinds of birds help plants reproduce by carrying pollen from one plant to another or by spreading their seeds.

This book shows you many of the different ways of life that birds have. Some of the birds you will read about will be those that you often see. You will find that when you know a little about a bird's way of life, it's a lot of fun to look for that bird. Perhaps you will see it do some of the things you have read about. Then you will begin to see how interesting bird watching can be!

Some of the birds in these pages are rare or *endangered* (at risk of becoming extinct, or dying without any survivors). Others are common. But each kind of bird is unique and special. Read on to find out why!

In addition to describing different birds in various habitats, this book includes poems about birds and instructions for some simple activities. At the back of *All About Birds*, you will find a list of Web sites and other books about birds. You will also find a glossary and an index.

What Is a Bird?

The Body of a Bird

What would it be like to feel lighter than air? What if you could lift your arms and rise into the sky, or leap off a cliff and *soar* (fly) on the wind? What if you could crack a nut with your teeth, sit on water, or grow decorations on your body? Birds can do all these things.

Some birds live in family groups, and others live alone. Some birds hunt mammals, fish, insects, or other birds. Others crack nuts or peck at seeds. Some birds soar for miles and miles, and others cannot fly at all. But all birds have wings, feathers, feet, and a bill. All these features help birds survive in places as different from one another as deserts, rain forests, and the Antarctic.

A wing is made of a few slim, hollow bones attached to powerful muscles in the bird's side. Thin skin and feathers cover each of a bird's wings.

Different birds use their wings in various ways. Soaring birds, such as the wandering albatross, have long, pointed wings that help them glide. Small, quick birds, like the chimney swift, have narrow wings that *taper* (become gradually smaller toward one end). Flightless penguins use their wings to help them swim,

During flight, the outer part of a bird's wing moves in a circular movement that begins on a full upstroke (1). It continues counterclockwise (2 and 3) through the downstroke and (4) at the start of another upstroke.

1   2   3   4

and ring-necked pheasants can use theirs to help them shoot up in the air and glide back down. Birds also use their wings for balance, to steer, and to fight.

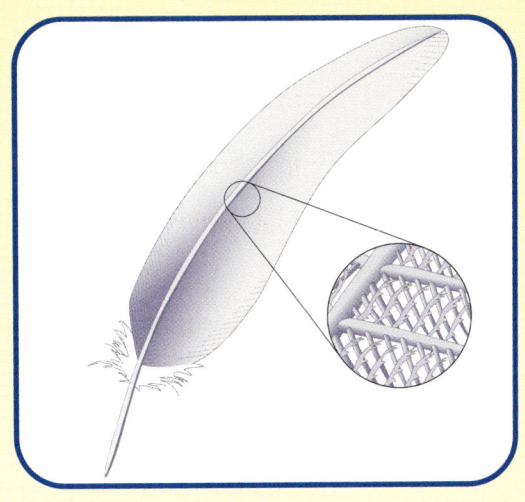

A bird's feathers also have many uses. Feathers can help catch the air currents that allow most birds to fly. They can also form a tight coat that holds in a bird's body heat. And feathers—which can be very decorative—may help birds attract mates or blend in with brush, flowers, fruits, or leaves. Some birds have *waterproof* feathers that allow them to dive and swim without becoming soaking wet.

A close-up view of the structure of a bird feather.

Feathers grow out of a bird's skin in the same way that hair grows out of a human's head. But unlike a person with a headful of hair, a bird *molts (mohltz)*— loses its old feathers and grows new ones—at least once a year. Some birds, such as the American goldfinch, molt twice a year. In the spring, goldfinches molt into their colorful breeding *plumage* (feathers), and in fall, they molt into less colorful plumage. Other birds, such as ducks and geese, molt all their flight feathers at the same time. After molting, these birds cannot fly until they grow new feathers.

Different birds have different kinds of feet. The feet of a bird are matched to its environment.

A superb lyrebird has long, trailing tail feathers.

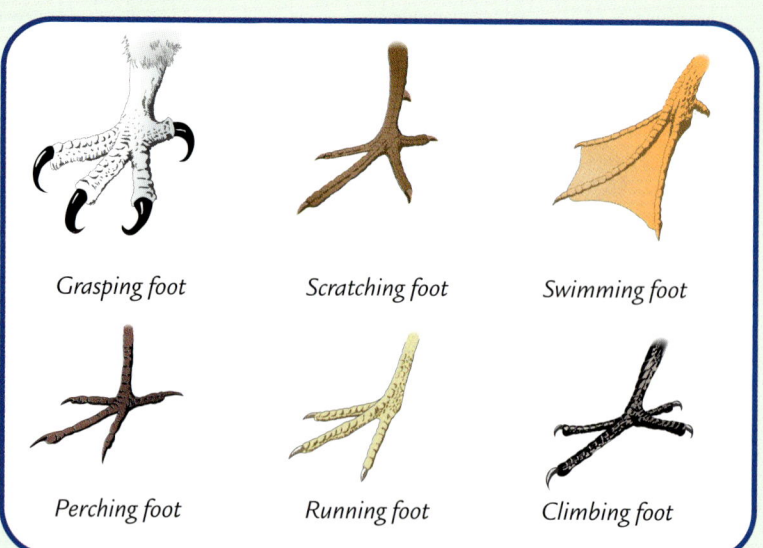

Grasping foot   Scratching foot   Swimming foot

Perching foot   Running foot   Climbing foot

The arrangement and size of a bird's toes and the shape of its claws varies, depending on the bird's way of life.

Perching birds, (belonging to the Passeriformes *order* [scientific grouping]) such as robins, sparrows, and jays have three long toes in front and one in back. This perching foot can grab a branch tightly—even when the bird is asleep. Woodpeckers have climbing feet that help to steady them as they climb. Birds of prey have grasping feet with large, curved claws—called *talons*— that they use for grabbing and killing their victims.

Birds that live on the ground have scratching feet, with short, blunt claws used to scratch for food. Some swimming birds, such as grebes *(greebz)*, have toes that act like paddles. Other swimming birds, such as ducks and swans, have webbed feet that work like swim fins.

Because birds eat so many different things, they have various kinds of bills. Seed-eating birds, such as finches and grosbeaks, have a stout, cracker bill that they use like a nutcracker. A woodpecker has a chisel bill that it uses to make a hole in a tree and find insects.

Chisel bill

Scoop bill

Cracker bill

Trap bill

Prober bill

Detector bill

The bills of birds vary, depending on what they eat and their feeding methods. Birds also use their bill in nest building and self-defense.

Other birds, such as the brown creeper, have a long, thin, prober bill that they use to dig into trees and probe for worms and insects.

A bird can use its bill for more than getting food. Many birds use their bill to *groom* themselves—that is, to smooth their feathers. Many birds also use their bill to grasp and carry materials for their nests and to arrange the materials in those nests.

A bird's tail does many important jobs. A bird may use its tail feathers to help it balance or to steer and land. Some birds, such as woodpeckers and sapsuckers, use their tail for support when they climb. Others, such as peacocks, have a tail that is a special ornament used to attract mates. A few birds—such as the kiwi, a flightless bird in New Zealand—do not have a tail.

The yellow-bellied sapsucker uses its tail as a prop when clinging to a tree trunk.

Bird Calls and Songs

It is a sunny spring morning, and the birds outside are busy. Sparrows are chirping noisily in a bush. They are keeping track of each other as they search for seeds. "I'm over here," calls each bird as it hops in, on, and around the bush. "Here I am!" "Now I'm here!" they seem to say.

A bright red cardinal is calling *wheet-chur, wheet-chur, wheet, wheet, wheet, wheet!* "This is my territory," the male cardinal warns. "Its boundaries are here, here, here, and here!" The cardinal's song tells other males to stay away — and at the same time, helps to attract a female cardinal as a mate.

In the distance, two crows are calling to each other. *Caw!* calls one. *Caw, Caw!* replies the other. These birds might be marking territory, like the cardinal, or warning each other about a hawk nearby. The crows may even be pointing out places to hunt for food.

Although bird calls may just sound like music to us, they are very useful to the birds. Not only do the calls keep individual birds safe, they also help keep large groups of birds, called *flocks,* together. And the calls allow birds to communicate—even from a distance. Almost every sound that birds make has a meaning. Some notes or calls translate into such words as "Danger!" or "Here I am!" Others may mean "I've found food." Many baby birds have a call that means, "Please feed me. I'm hungry!"

Some birds can sing long songs, which are much more complex than simple calls. Male birds may use their beautiful songs to impress female birds. If a female is impressed enough, she will go to the male, and the two birds will become mates.

About half of the known *species* (kinds) of birds, including nearly all perching birds, make both calls and songs. Most other kinds of birds, including most water birds and birds of prey, call but do not sing.

Pelicans and some storks are among the few birds that have no voice. Male and female storks clatter their bills at one another to communicate. Some birds make snapping sounds with their wings or drumming rhythms with their bill on a tree to communicate. Still other birds communicate by visual displays such as flashing their tail feathers.

Prep and Caring

Every year, usually in the spring, adult birds look for a mate. Once a male and a female have paired up, they make or find a nest, where the mother bird will lay her eggs after mating. The nest is also a kind of "nursery" where the mother or father—or both birds—take care of the young.

Different birds make different kinds of nests. Many birds build a nest in a tree. Some tree nests are simple platforms. Other nests, such as those of some swallows, are bowls or hanging pouches of grass, mud, and twigs. Woodpeckers dig a hole in a tree, which they use as a nest. Other birds make their nest on the ground or in a hole in the ground. Some kinds of water birds build a nest that floats like a raft.

Each egg a mother bird lays contains tiny cells that may grow into a baby bird. An egg also contains a golden-orange *yolk*, which is food for the growing bird. The mother or father bird *incubates (IHN kyuh baytz)*, or keeps the egg warm, as the baby bird grows. Sometimes the parents take turns crouching over the egg until it hatches. Once their egg is laid, some kinds of birds can hatch from their egg in fewer than two weeks. Others keep growing inside the egg for more than two months before hatching.

A swallow builds a hanging nest under a beam.

A yellow warbler feeding her chicks.

Many baby birds have a sharp, little bump on their bill. When a fully grown baby wiggles and squirms within the egg, the bump scrapes against the inside of the shell and makes cracks and holes in it. Soon the egg breaks open, and the baby bird is born.

Altricial (al TRIHSH uhl) birds, including baby hummingbirds, pelicans, and all songbirds, are weak and helpless at first. They are born unable to see and practically featherless. So the mother or father *broods* (crouches over) these baby birds to keep them warm and safe. *Precocial (prih KOH shuhl)* birds, including baby chickens, ducks, turkeys, and swans, are born with a soft coat of feathers, called *down*. These birds can see and walk almost as soon as they are born.

Helpless or not, most birds either stay in the nest or, if precocial, remain with their parents until they are grown. One or both parents feed them and teach them how to hunt, fly, and hide from enemies. When they are ready, the young birds go out into the world to explore, mate, and raise their own families.

Ways to Stay Safe

Different kinds of *predators* (animals that kill other animals for food) hunt for birds on land, in the sea, and in the air. But birds have ways to protect themselves from their enemies. They use three main forms of protection—hiding, flying, and fighting.

Many birds have coloring and markings that help *camouflage (KAM uh flahzh)* them. This means they are able to hide by blending in with their environment. Their feathers create patterns and shadows that blend in with grasses, leaves, and twigs. Some *tropical* (warm-area) birds have brightly colored feathers that help them look like a flower or a fruit.

A bird will try to hide or fly away to safety if it spots a predator. But if the predator gets too close, the bird may have to fight. It may use its bill, legs, or wings to fight off an enemy. Often it will call loudly at an intruder and fly at its head. By fighting this way, birds have a chance against predatory birds and other animals their own size. But they usually cannot win against bigger creatures.

If a predator happens to come near a bird's nesting place on the ground, a mother or father bird might trick the predator, to draw it away from the nest. The parent may drag a wing on the ground or walk oddly so that it looks as if it is injured. The predator will follow the "injured" bird away from the nest. When both the bird and the predator are far from the nest, the mother or father bird will simply fly away.

The feathers of a rock ptarmigan help to camouflage it.

Twice a Year Trip

Twice each year, millions of birds leave one home and fly to another home in a different part of the world. When it is fall in the northern part of the world, many birds fly south where food is more plentiful. Six months later, these birds fly back north when food is again easier to find. This journey is called *migration (my GRAY shuhn)*, which means moving from one place to another.

Migration is an amazing process. It requires a knowledge of when seasons are changing and when food might become scarce. Migration also requires

A flock of snow geese taking flight.

strength and an ability to *navigate* (steer) over great distances. Yet many kinds of birds, both large and small, manage to migrate every year.

Not all birds migrate. Some birds live in the same place all year long because their *habitat* (natural living place) has enough food and water for them. But migrating birds must travel to and from the same places each year.

Some birds migrate in flocks. Others make the journey alone. Some birds fly only at night, and

others fly by day. Most birds make stops along their migration route in order to rest or find food. A few kinds of birds fly without stopping until they reach their destination.

Whether they travel only a few hundred miles or several thousands of miles over mountains, plains, and seas, most migrating birds use the sun, moon, and stars to help them find their way. Scientists believe that many migrating birds may also be guided by Earth's *magnetic field*, a field of magnetic force created by the planet.

Studying and Protecting

Ornithologists (or nih THOL uh juhsts) are scientists who study birds. But they are not the only ones who take note of these fascinating creatures. Millions of people are bird watchers. Many of them use *binoculars (bin OK yuh luhrz)* —two small telescopes attached side by side so a person can use both eyes at once to look at things that are far away—to see birds high in the trees or sky. But other bird watchers simply use their eyes to enjoy birds at backyard feeders.

One way to be a bird watcher is to go to fields, wetlands, and forests where a lot of birds live. Find a good spot, sit very still, and then wait for birds. More serious bird watchers may want to build a hiding place, which is sometimes called a *blind*. Blinds range from simple tents that blend in with their surroundings to complex sheds with special windows. Even a car can be used as a blind. Once birds get used to seeing a blind in their habitat, they will begin to ignore it.

Pine cone feeders and suet cakes also attract birds.

Another way to find birds to study is to attract them to the place where you live. Many birds like to eat corn or the seeds of such plants as hemp, sunflower, and millet. You can also buy wild bird seed or "chicken scratch" from a supermarket, pet shop, or feed store. Bacon pieces, apple cores, orange segments, shelled unsalted peanuts, and water-soaked raisins are also foods that birds enjoy.

A pine cone feeder or a *suet (SOO iht)* cake should also attract birds. Suet is a hard animal fat. It provides the extra food energy birds need during cold weather.

To make a **pine cone feeder**, spread peanut butter on a pine cone, roll it in seeds or nuts, then hang the pine cone outdoors. To make a **suet cake**, ask an adult to help you melt 2 ounces (59 milliliters) of lard over low heat in a pan. Then stir in 2 ounces of wild bird seed. Carefully pour the mixture into a plastic container and push one end of a string into the container. Cool the mixture, pop it out of the container, and use the string to hang it outdoors.

Birds don't just eat, they drink too! If you fill clay-pot saucers or bird baths with water, birds are likely to

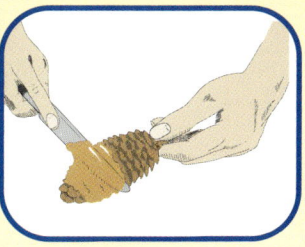

1. First, spread peanut butter on a pine cone.

2. Next, roll the pine cone in seeds or nuts. Then hang your pine cone feeder outside.

Suet cake—*ask an adult to help you.*

1. Add bird seed to melted suet.

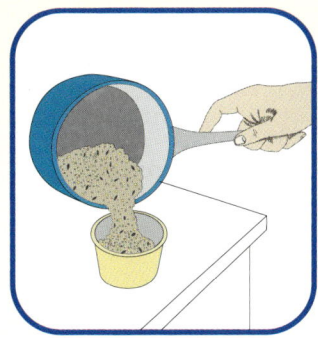

2. Pour the mixture into a container.

3. Place a string into the mixture and let it cool.

23

August 3 AT 8 AM
WOODS BEHIND MY HOUSE

OVENBIRD:
OLIVE
GREEN
ORANGE &
BLACK STRIPES

TAIL
RAISED
BLACK &
WHITE
UNDERNEATH

August 7 AT 3 PM
BIRD FEEDER
IN MY BACKYARD

SAW
CARDINAL
BLUE JAY
ROBIN

CARDINALS:

Keep records of birds you have seen in a bird journal.

stop by to visit. But be sure to change the water frequently.

Many bird watchers like to keep records of the birds they have seen. To keep a bird journal, write the date and your *location* (the place where you saw the birds) at the top of a page each time you go bird watching. List the birds that you see. Jot down the time at which you saw the birds and what they were doing. When you see a bird you do not recognize, take a picture of it, make a sketch of it, or describe it in words. Pay attention to such details as the shape of the bird's bill, feet, tail, and wings, and record the parts of the body where you saw patches of color. Later on, look up the bird in a field guide.

You may want to decorate your bird journal by coloring your sketches and adding other pictures. You can also transfer your records to index cards or into a computer file.

Making a Birdhouse

You can attract some kinds of birds to your backyard by making a **birdhouse.** If you put the birdhouse up in early spring, you will attract birds that are returning from their winter homes. Make sure an adult helps you with this project.

You can make a birdhouse out of a one quart (.95 liter) milk carton. First, prepare the carton. Open up the carton at the top, wash and dry the inside, and then spray the inside with black paint. (Birds prefer to nest in dark places.) After it dries, reclose the carton with duct tape.

Next, design the house. Punch two drainage holes in the bottom of the carton with a sharpened pencil. Then turn the carton on its side and make four more holes— one in each corner, about 2 inches (5 centimeters) from the edge. On the side of the carton opposite to these holes, use scissors to cut a round doorway no more than 1 ¼ inches (3 centimeters) wide. You can paint the house green or brown to blend in with the tree. Or paint it white to reflect the sun and keep the house cool.

Finally, choose the tree where you want to hang the house. A spot shaded from the sun is best. Cut two pieces of wire long enough to wrap securely around the tree. Thread one piece of wire through the top two holes of the birdhouse and the other piece through the bottom two holes. Fasten the house securely to the tree.

Endangered Birds

An endangered nene, also called a Hawaiian goose, in Maui, Hawaii.

Some birds are very common. Others are rare. Some are so rare that they are considered *threatened* or *endangered*. This means that some bird species are at risk of becoming *extinct* —dying out without any survivors.

Loss of habitat is the main threat to birds today. Many birds are endangered because people have taken over the land on which the birds live, including land used during migration. Hunters have killed large numbers of birds. Still other birds, such as the California condor, have suffered from illegal egg collecting, as well as from hunting and loss of habitat.

Pollution has killed many kinds of birds. Certain *pesticides* (substances used to kill insects and other pests), such as DDT, poisoned the food of many ospreys, bald eagles, pelicans, and peregrine falcons. After eating the poisoned food, these birds laid eggs that had such thin shells that they cracked when the parents tried to incubate them. Restrictions on certain kinds of pollution have helped many birds to recover. Scientists have also raised some birds in *captivity* (places removed from the wild). The offspring of these birds have then been released into the wild.

Peregrine falcons have recovered so well that they are no longer considered endangered. However, other birds, such as whooping cranes, have not yet recovered fully and continue to need extra help and protection.

In North America, the West Nile virus has killed many kinds of crows and other birds. A mosquito carries the virus. If a mosquito bites a bird, the bird can become ill and die. Mosquitoes can also give the virus to humans. The virus was once found only in tropical lands. Some scientists believe infected birds that migrated to new areas spread the virus. Other scientists think mosquitoes carrying the virus found their way to the new areas. To protect birds from this virus, people try to reduce the number of mosquitoes.

Many governments have made treaties and other agreements to protect endangered birds from human activities. Some have set up refuges to protect birds. As the human population continues to grow, many birds may die unless scientists and others continue to work hard to ensure them a place to live and food to eat.

Sandhill cranes and an endangered whooping crane feeding in a field.

27

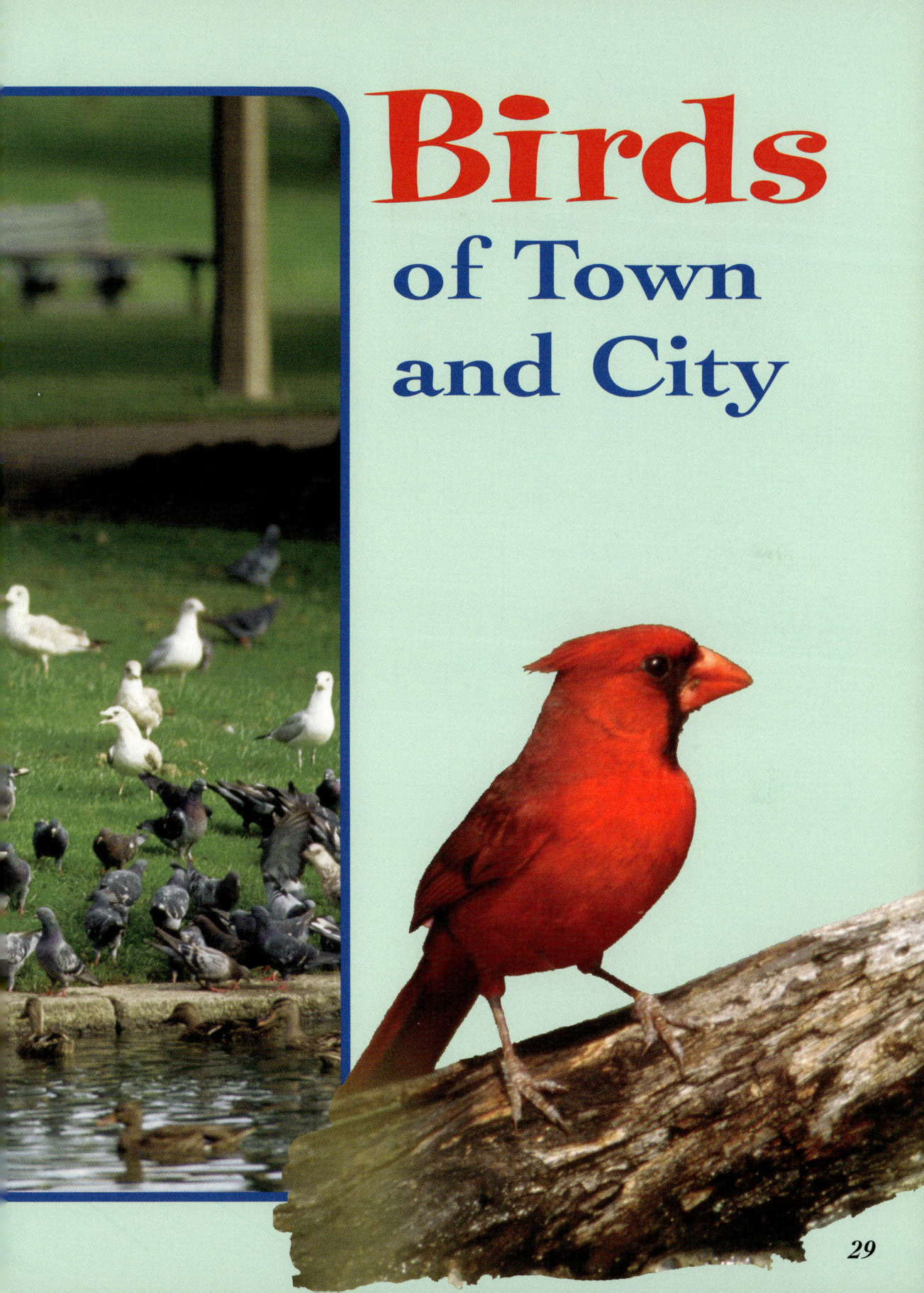

Birds

of Town and City

The First Sign of Spring

It was a bright morning in early April. In a small forest, the last icy patches of winter snow were melting away. The lawns of a nearby town were fresh and green. Trees were beginning to bud.

A blur of red and brown sailed through the air and landed on the roof of a house. It was a plump bird with a brown back and wings and a brick-red breast—a male American robin. The robin cocked a bright, beady eye toward the lawn to see if any earthworms were about. Then he opened his bill and sang.

"Cheerily, cheer-up, cheerio!"

In the house next door, a little boy heard the song. He looked out of a window, saw the robin, and grinned. It was the first robin he'd seen this year—and that meant winter was over! Like many Americans, he believed that the robin was a sure sign of spring.

Within a few days, the male robin was joined by a female. Soon, she began to build a nest. She picked out

Photographs on pages 28—29

Pigeons in the Public Garden in Boston, Massachusetts, and a Northern cardinal.

a place among the branches of a large evergreen shrub that sprawled under the kitchen window of a house. It was well hidden from any birds that might fly overhead, as well as from people who might pass by. It was also too high for a dog's curious nose to poke into and in too hard a place for a cat to get at.

The female began by making a platform of twigs and grass on a branch. Then, using her bill to move grass and mud—and sometimes bits of string, cloth, or paper that she found on lawns and sidewalks—she built up the sides of the nest. The mud dried and held everything together.

When the sides and bottom were thick and firm, the robin filled her bill with mud. She smeared the mud all over the inside of the nest. Then she squatted in the

nest and turned around several times. This smoothed the mud and gave the inside of the nest a bowl shape. The robin then lined the inside of the nest with soft grass. Now, everything was ready.

Within a few days, she had laid four pale blue eggs in the bottom of the nest. She spent most of the next dozen days squatting upon the eggs to keep them warm so they would hatch. She left the nest only for short times, to hunt for food. During this period, her mate, the male robin, stayed nearby to guard her and the eggs.

Finally, four tiny, scrawny baby robins hatched out of the eggs. They were completely helpless. Their eyes were closed, and they were too weak to move. They had no feathers, so their mother had to *brood* them (crouch over them) to keep them warm.

The father robin helped to find food for the baby robins. All day long he searched for worms, beetles, grasshoppers, and other such creatures. When he found something, he flew back to the nest at once. He always landed on or near the nest, which made it jiggle. This movement of the nest told the baby robins that food had come.

At once, each small robin stretched out its neck and opened its mouth as wide as it could! The father stuffed food into the mouth of the little bird that seemed hungriest. Then he flew off in search of another worm or insect.

In about a week, the young robins' eyes were open. They began to grow fluffy coats of feathers. Now they didn't need to be brooded as often, so the mother robin could leave her nest more often.

About two weeks after hatching, the young robins had all their feathers. But they didn't look exactly like their mother and father. Instead of having orange or red breasts, the young robins' breasts were tan-colored and speckled with dark spots. As they grew older, their breasts would turn orange or red.

By the time the youngsters began trying to fly, their mother had flown off to build another nest and raise another family. The father stayed behind to look after the young ones.

This was a dangerous time for them. A cat or other enemy might easily catch them. But, before long, they became good fliers and were safe. Once they could fly, they went off by themselves.

During the next few months, the mother robin and father robin might have one or two more families. All summer long, red-breasted adults and speckle-breasted youngsters would be a common sight running about on lawns.

But, by late autumn, the redbreasts would be gone from the northern parts of the country. They would move far enough south to avoid the snow and bitter cold. Then, when winter was over, they would be among the first birds to return, a sign that spring had come again.

Chimney Dwellers

Chimney swifts are rather small birds, only about 5 inches (13 centimeters) long. They are well named, for they often rest and build their nests inside chimneys. And they certainly are swift, for they are among the fastest of all birds.

Except when sleeping or keeping eggs warm, chimney swifts spend almost all their time flying. They rarely *perch* (sit) in trees and never run about on the ground. They get all their food while they fly—opening up their wide mouths to gulp down flying insects they catch in midair. They even build their nests as they fly, without once *alighting* (coming down from flight).

To make a nest, the swifts break small, dead twigs off trees. They fly at the twigs and snap them off by hitting them with their feet. Then they carry the twigs in their bills to a chimney—or perhaps a hollow tree. They glue the twigs to the inside wall of the chimney with their *saliva* (spit), which is thick and sticky. They glue more twigs together to form a nest that looks like half a basket sticking out from the wall.

When a chimney swift rests inside a chimney, it can't perch on a branch as a robin does because its legs and feet are small and weak. The swift digs its sharp toes into the side of the chimney. To keep from sliding down, it uses its tail as a prop.

At *migration* time (the time when birds move to a different area to find more food or a better climate), whole flocks of these little birds will often rest inside a

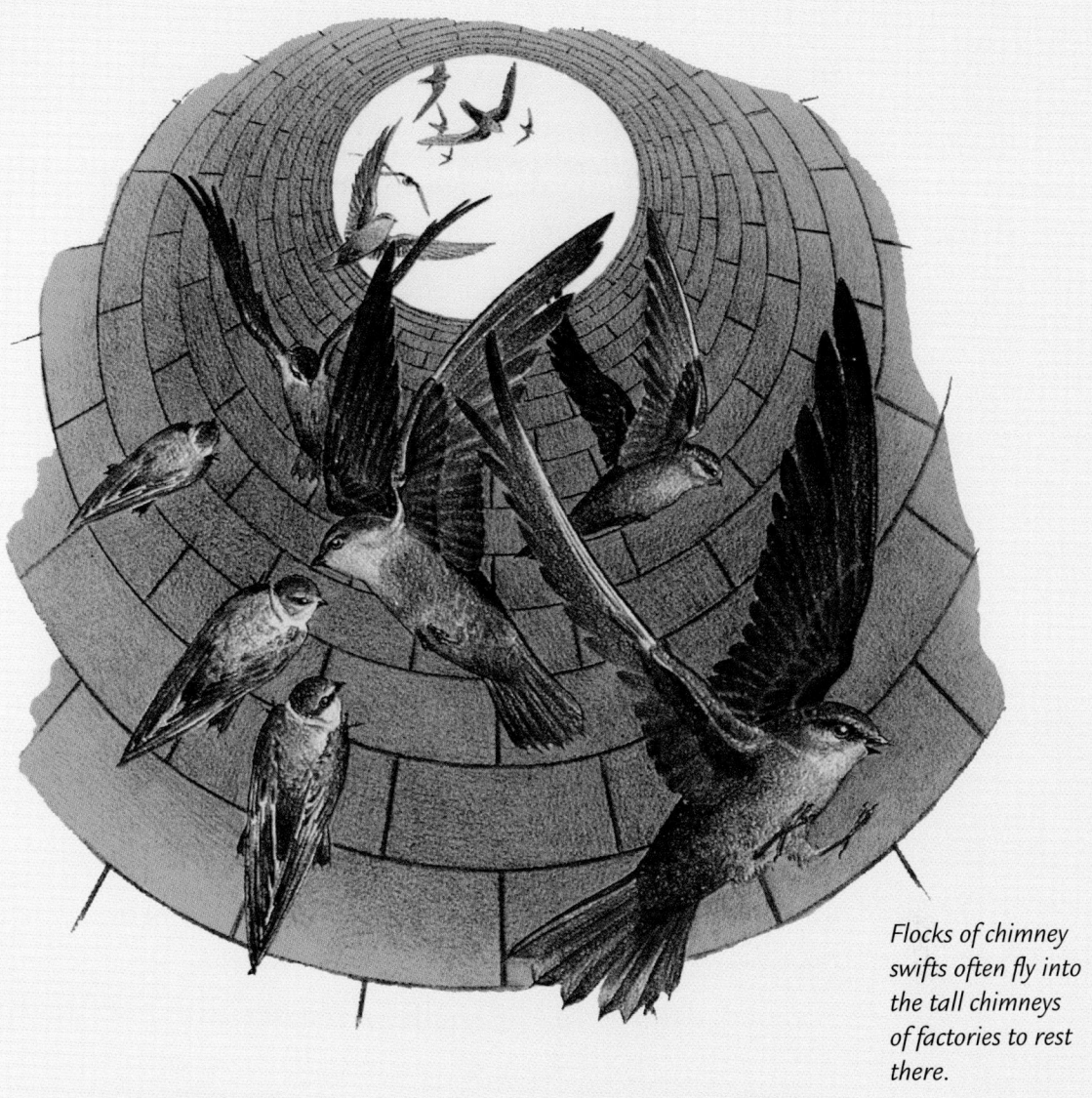

Flocks of chimney swifts often fly into the tall chimneys of factories to rest there.

tall factory chimney. They fly around the chimney in a ring for a while. Then, some birds circle down into the chimney. More and more follow. The circle begins to look like a funnel-shaped cloud of smoke—but a cloud that's going down into the chimney instead of rising out of it! 🍃

Apartment Dwellers

Purple martins have been on friendly terms with people for a long time. North American Indians used to hang hollow gourds in which purple martins made their homes. The martins chased away nearby crows and other birds that raided the Indians' crops. Today, many North Americans put up big "apartment houses" in which martins can nest.

Martins like to live in a large group, called a *colony*. Before each pair of birds in a colony chooses an "apartment" and builds a nest, martins do a lot of bustling about and "arguing." The birds fight over who gets the best nesting areas. When the eggs begin to hatch in the spring, there's great excitement. The parents take turns feeding the young with flies, mosquitoes, and even wasps.

By late August or early September, the young are full-grown fliers. The martins leave their apartment houses and join each other in the air. Together, they form huge flocks and fly south for the winter.

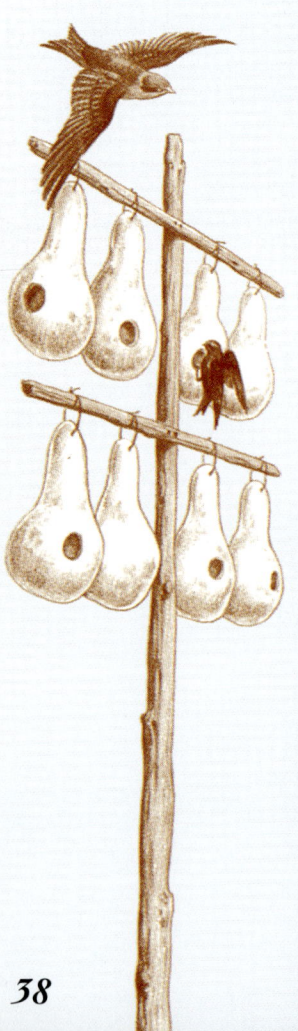

Hollow gourds hung to house purple martins (below) and a large "apartment building" to house martins (right).

Skyscraper Dwellers

The city birds we call pigeons are really a kind of bird known as a rock dove. Wild rock doves usually live on cliffs by the sea and make their nests in caves.

City pigeons carry on their lives in the middle of the city's noise, smoke, and bustle. They build their nests on the ledges of skyscrapers and on the *girders* (beams) of bridges.

When baby pigeons hatch, their eyes are closed and they are helpless. But adult pigeons are able to make a milky, fatty sort of liquid inside of their throat. The mother and father pigeons feed this liquid, called crop milk, to the baby pigeons by dribbling it down the baby pigeons' throats.

A pigeon sits on the ledge of a skyscraper.

As the young pigeons, or squabs (*skwahbz*), grow older, their parents bring them fruit, grains, caterpillars, and other things to eat. After four or five weeks, the young ones are out on their own—waddling around the city, looking for something to eat.

City pigeons are friendly birds. Sometimes, however, they carry diseases. Many people regard them as serious pests.

39

A Nest on a Rooftop

In many parts of Europe, people invite a bird to make its nest on their roof! They'll even put a big basket or a platform on the roof, on which the bird can build its nest.

The bird they welcome is the big white stork. People in the Netherlands, Germany, Austria, and other parts of Europe feel that storks living on the roof will bring good luck. So, they are glad to have storks nest on their roofs.

The storks spend the winter in Africa and India. In the springtime, they fly back to Europe. The male storks usually show up first. A male will pick out a good place for a nest, such as a chimney, a roof, a church tower, or even a telephone pole. There, he waits until a female stork comes to join him. Together, they build a nest.

A stork nest is a huge pile of sticks, grass, and other plant materials woven together. Sometimes, a pair of storks will take over an old nest and build it up even higher. The storks collect their building material from the streets and fields. Sometimes, a stork will even steal a piece of clothing from a clothesline to use in building its nest!

When the female has laid all her eggs, she and the male take turns sitting on the eggs so they will hatch. The first baby storks hatch after about 32 days. Both the mother and father bring them food, which at first is mostly worms. When the young birds are about eight weeks old, they begin to practice flying. They flap their wings and make little jumps. In a few more weeks, they can fly.

Storks eat insects, fish, frogs, lizards, snakes, mice, rats, and other small creatures. They get their food by walking about in fields or wading in swamps, snapping up anything they find.

There is a legend that young storks feed and take care of their parents. But this isn't true. In fact, young storks migrate to Africa or India in late summer, leaving their parents behind. The parents follow about two weeks later.

Storks nesting on top of a church in Poland.

Noisy Neighbors

The common, or European, starling has black feathers with a greenish-purple gloss. At one time, there were no starlings in North America. But in the early 1890's, about 100 starlings from Europe were set free in New York City's Central Park. Today, the bird is a common sight strutting on lawns and *roosting* (sitting) on buildings throughout America.

Starlings are noisy, pushy birds! They'll shove other birds aside to get food. They even steal food when they can. Suppose a starling and a robin are hunting on the same lawn. If the robin finds a worm, the starling may rush over and take the worm right out of the robin's bill! It's surprising, but the robin seldom puts up a fuss.

Starlings will also push other birds out of their nests and take over the nests for themselves. Starlings like to nest in holes in tree trunks or in small openings in the walls of houses and buildings. They'll also nest in a birdhouse, which they stuff with a padding of sticks, straws, dried grass, or even wastepaper.

Almost every city in North America and Europe has a lot of starlings. These bold little birds often roost by the dozen on window ledges, trees, and even inside large, open public buildings. Many people look upon starlings as pests. Starlings often chatter, squeak, and whistle all night long, keeping people awake. And they are rather messy.

In many places, people have tried to get rid of starlings. But nothing has worked. The starlings seem quite happy and able to live alongside people—whether the people want them or not!

Other Birds
of Town and City

Blue jay
11 to 12 ½ inches
(28 to 32 centimeters)

House wren
4 ½ to 5 ¼ inches
(11 to 13.3 centimeters)

Northern mockingbird
9 to 11 inches
(23 to 28 centimeters)

Northern cardinal
7 to 9 inches
(18 to 23 centimeters)

House sparrow
5 ½ to 6 ¼ inches
(14 to 16 centimeters)

Birds

of Farmland and Open Country

A Trickster

It was springtime. A large black-and-white cat trotted across the farm field. Suddenly, she stopped in the middle of a step, as cats do, with one paw off the ground. She had seen something.

A bird lay on the ground ahead of her. It was a fairly large bird, about 10 inches (25 centimeters) long, with a brownish back and wings and a white breast that had two dark bands at the neck. It seemed sick, or hurt. It was panting and gasping, weakly.

The cat became interested. She took a few cautious steps toward the bird. At once, the bird gave a shrill shriek and began to flutter away. It dragged one wing on the ground, as if it might be broken. It shrieked again. The cat stopped and stared. The bird also stopped and lay panting and shrieking.

The cat flattened herself against the ground and began to creep forward. The bird fluttered away,

Photographs on pages 46—47

A ring-necked pheasant in a field of grasses and a barn swallow resting on a plant.

helplessly, giving screams of fear. Another bird now appeared overhead, shrieking loudly. It was the first bird's mate. Apparently, it was trying to help the injured bird by getting the cat's attention so that the other bird could escape.

But the cat paid no attention. She sensed an easy victory and speeded up her movement toward the prey. The injured bird managed to keep fluttering and flopping away from her. But, surely, the cat would catch up to the poor creature before long!

Farther and farther across the field they went, the cat pursuing the frightened, fluttering bird. But, suddenly, the bird stopped shrieking. Calmly, it spread its wings, flew up into the air, and headed back across the field!

Birds of Farmland and Open Country

The cat stared after it for a moment. Then she sat down and began to lick her paw. She seemed to be trying to show that she didn't care if the bird had escaped—and didn't care if she had been fooled into believing it was hurt and helpless!

The bird skimmed over the field and came down just about where the cat had first seen it. Four baby birds hurried to it. It was their mother. The cat might have discovered these young birds. But when the mother acted as if she had a broken wing, she tricked the cat into following her far away. This is how these birds, which are called killdeers, protect their eggs and their young.

Killdeers got their name because of the sound they often make—*kil-deeer, kil-deeer*. They belong to a family of birds that usually lives along shores. They live mostly in North and South America, but they are sometimes seen in western Europe. Killdeers like to live in open meadows and fields. They especially like plowed farm fields, where there are plenty of insects. They're good friends to farmers, because they eat lots of the kinds of insects that damage farm crops.

Killdeers are not the only kind of birds that protect their young by pretending to be hurt. Many other kinds of birds that make their nests on the ground also play this "trick."

Ostriches live in flocks in the dry parts of Africa. They are the biggest of all birds.

The Biggest Birds

The world's three biggest types of birds live on huge, flat, open plains: The tallest lives in Africa, the second tallest in Australia, and the third in South America. These birds look a lot alike and live in much the same way. None of them can fly, but they all can run quickly on their two sturdy legs.

The biggest of all living birds is the ostrich of Africa. A male ostrich may be as much as 8 feet (2.4 meters) tall. This bird may weigh as much as 345 pounds (156 kilograms).

Despite its size, this big, heavy bird runs very fast. An ostrich can run 40 miles (64 kilometers) an hour. That's almost as fast as a race horse can run. Baby ostriches can run soon after they hatch.

It isn't true that an ostrich will try to hide by burying its head in the sand. However, an ostrich will often bend its neck down and use its bill to rearrange its eggs on the ground. From a distance, the head seems to disappear.

The male ostrich is a good father. He makes the nest by scooping out a shallow pit in the sand. He then sits down in it. The eggs are laid in front of him, and he pushes them under his body. He then *incubates* the eggs (keeps them warm so they will hatch) each day.

The emu *(EE myoo)* lives mostly in woodlands and on dry plains in Australia. It is about 5 to 6 feet (1.5 to 1.8 meters) tall and weighs about 100 pounds (45 kilograms).

The rhea *(REE uh)* lives on grassy plains in South America. Rheas are about 5 feet (1.5 meters) tall and weigh about 50 pounds (23 kilograms). Father rheas and emus do all the work of taking care of their young. They make the nests and incubate the eggs. When the baby birds hatch, the fathers stay with them until the young birds can take care of themselves.

A male rhea.

Long-Legged Hunter

A very tall bird stalked through clumps of yellow-green grass on the African plain. The bird marched with great dignity on two long, slim legs. As it walked, it peered at the ground. From time to time, it stomped one foot noisily. When a startled grasshopper leaped up into the air, the bird gulped it down.

Then the bird stomped and startled—a deadly, poisonous snake! The cobra reared up to challenge the bird. But the bird simply flicked one wing in front of itself like a shield. It stomped on the snake until the cobra was dead. Then it picked up the snake in its bill and swallowed it! The long-legged secretary-bird eats lizards and insects in addition to poisonous snakes.

Secretary-birds can fly, but they seldom do. They spend most of their time walking over grassy plains. They walk about as fast as a human. But that's not why they are called secretary-birds.

Here's one idea about how the secretary-bird got its name. A secretary is a person whose work is to write letters and keep records of things. In the 1700's, secretaries were men who wore white powdered wigs. They wrote with quill pens made from feathers. When a secretary needed a place to put his pens, he sometimes stuck them in the back of his wig. This elegant African bird has tufts of feathers sticking out of the back of its head, too—and perhaps that reminded some explorers of the secretaries back home.

A secretary-bird.

Hitchhiking Bird

You might think that it would annoy an animal to have birds walking on it and pecking it with their sharp bills. But when oxpeckers land on an antelope, a giraffe, or a rhinoceros, the animals usually are glad!

An oxpecker doesn't ride about on an animal just for fun. It does it because that's how the oxpecker gets its food. The bird walks over an animal, searching for ticks and other insects, many of which burrow into the animal's skin. The oxpecker gobbles up these pesky creatures.

A red-billed oxpecker on a type of African antelope called an impala.

Oxpeckers don't stay only with wild animals. They also live on tame cattle that belong to farmers' herds. At night, an oxpecker may leave its animal and fly up into a nearby tree to roost. But, usually, it will stay with the animal, even when that animal lies down to sleep. By staying with it, the bird won't have to search for a new place to eat in the morning!

A Borrowed Burrow

The sun is setting on a prairie in North America. On a little hump of earth, in front of a hole, stands a small, long-legged owl. Slowly, it turns its head almost all the way around in a circle. Its wide eyes peer carefully over the prairie.

In the distance, a coyote trots along, heading straight toward the owl. The owl makes a sort of bowing motion several times. Then it pops into the hole and vanishes from sight. The coyote trots on.

This kind of owl is known as a burrowing owl. Its home and hiding place is an underground tunnel. Usually, a burrowing owl takes over an empty hole or burrow some other animal has made, such as a tortoise hole or prairie dog burrow. If it can't find such a place, it digs its own, with its feet and beak.

A burrowing owl catches a mouse.

Like all other kinds of owls, burrowing owls are meat-eaters. They hunt at night and sometimes in the daylight. They run along the ground to catch land animals and hope to snatch insects out of the air. When they're flying, they dive to snatch small creatures on the ground. They'll eat beetles, grasshoppers, small birds, ground squirrels, mice, and other small animals.

Burrowing owls stand in front of a burrow.

At mating time, the male prepares a nest in a burrow, using dried plants, feathers, and cow manure. The female stays with her eggs while the male guards her from a nearby burrow and brings her food. When the eggs hatch, the mother and father owls transfer the young to several nearby burrows. That way, if an enemy attacks one burrow, the baby owls—called *owlets*—in the other burrows will be safe.

The Prairie Hawk

A large bird circled low over a farm field in western North America. The bird was all white except for its legs and the back of its wings, which were reddish-brown. It was a ferruginous *(fuh ROO juh nuhs)* hawk. These hawks are named for the color of their legs and wings. The word *ferruginous* means "reddish-brown" or "rust-colored."

The field had just been harvested. The green plants were all gone. Only the dark dirt remained. The hawk seemed to be studying the field.

In a few moments, the bird saw what it was looking for. Some of the dirt had been pushed up into little piles by gophers *(GOH fuhrz)* — small, ratlike animals that live in underground tunnels.

The hawk glided down. Softly as a feather falling into snow, it landed by one of the piles. For a time, it

waited. Then, there was a stirring in the earth. A new pile of dirt started to form. A gopher was working just beneath the surface.

In an instant, the hawk opened its wings and rose a short way into the air. Then it dropped. Its feet stabbed into the pile of dirt. A moment later it flapped up into the air, the body of the gopher dangling from its claws. The gopher never knew what hit it. It was killed instantly by the hawk's grip.

Ferruginous hawks are about 2 feet (61 centimeters) long. They are birds of the prairies and farmlands. They are a help to farmers, as they eat mainly gophers, ground squirrels, and prairie dogs — all animals that damage crops.

Bird "Criminals"

Spring has come to the English countryside. A gray-bodied cuckoo with a gray-and-white-striped breast is moving in the field, looking for the nest of a reed warbler. After a time, she finds one—a loose bowl of grass and twigs among the low branches of a bush. The female warbler is on the nest. She has laid one egg and will lay more in the days to come.

The female cuckoo lurks nearby. When the warbler leaves for a few moments, the cuckoo flies straight to the nest and lays an egg. Then she picks up the warbler egg in her bill and flies away.

Soon, the warbler returns. She sits on the egg as if it were hers. Over the next several days, she lays the rest of her eggs.

The cuckoo egg hatches first. At first, the baby cuckoo seems weak and helpless. It has no feathers,

and its eyes are closed. It doesn't move or make a
sound. The mother warbler leaves the nest in search of
food for the baby.

Then, several hours later, the baby cuckoo begins to
wiggle around the bottom of the nest. When it comes
to an egg, the cuckoo burrows down beneath it. Then
it pushes upward—until the egg falls out of the nest!
The baby cuckoo keeps wiggling and burrowing,
burrowing and pushing, until it is all alone in the nest.

When the mother warbler returns to the nest, she
does not notice the missing eggs. All she thinks about
is the baby bird in the nest that is begging for food.
She devotes herself to feeding the baby cuckoo, which
gets bigger and fatter each day.

A cuckoo bird.

Every year, in many parts of the world, birds become "foster" parents to baby cuckoos, cowbirds, and some other kinds of birds that lay their eggs in the nests of other birds. The mothers of these baby birds don't always choose warblers to be foster parents. But they usually choose a kind of bird whose eggs look similar to their own. Sometimes, the foster parent is a much smaller bird than the birth mother—so the baby towers over its foster parent!

The mother cuckoos and their young don't mean any harm; they're just following their *instincts* (things that animals know without having been taught). Those instincts put other baby birds in danger, but they do help the cuckoos and others find a good mother for their young.

The cuckoo is a giddy bird,
No other is as she,
That flits across the meadow,
That sings in every tree.
A nest she never buildeth,
A vagrant she doth roam;
Her music is but tearful —
Cuckoo — cuckoo — cuckoo!
"I nowhere have a home."

from *The Cuckoo*
Author unknown

A hedge sparrow (left) feeds a young cuckoo.

Budgies

The sprightly, little birds that many people call parakeets, and keep as pets, are actually budgerigars *(buhj uhr ee GAHRZ)*, or budgies. In Australia, they live in the wild in large, noisy flocks on vast grassy plains dotted here and there with trees. They eat mostly grass seed. When the seed in one place is eaten up, the flock flies to a new place. Thus, budgerigars are often on the move.

But life is not always easy on the grassland. Sometimes, no rain falls for many months and waterholes dry up. The flocks must then fly in search of water. If none is found soon enough, hundreds of thousands of the little birds might perish.

However, budgies are fitted for such a life.
They are able to go for days without drinking,
as long as they have enough ripe seeds to eat.
After a drought, the birds can breed quickly with
the onset of rain.

After a rainfall, flocks of budgies gather in
the branches of mallee scrub trees. There are so
many green birds on each branch, the tree looks
as if it had burst into blossom with greenery.
Pairs of birds crawl about the branches
looking for cracks. Using their bills, they chip
away at these cracks to make them bigger.
The holes they make then become nests in
which the females lay their eggs.

The word budgerigar comes from the language of
the Aborigines, the first people who lived in Australia.
Long ago, the Aborigines hunted budgies for food.

Other **Birds**
of Farmland and Open Country

Barn swallow
About 7 ½ inches
(19 centimeters)

Western kingbird
8 to 9 ½ inches
(20 to 24 centimeters)

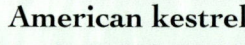

American kestrel
About 8 inches
(20 centimeters)

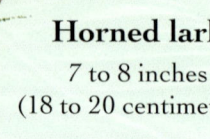

Horned lark
7 to 8 inches
(18 to 20 centimeters)

Eastern meadowlark
8 to 9 inches
(20 to 23 centimeters)

Dickcissel
6 to 7 inches
(15 to 18 centimeters)

Magpie
18 to 19 inches
(46 to 48 centimeters)

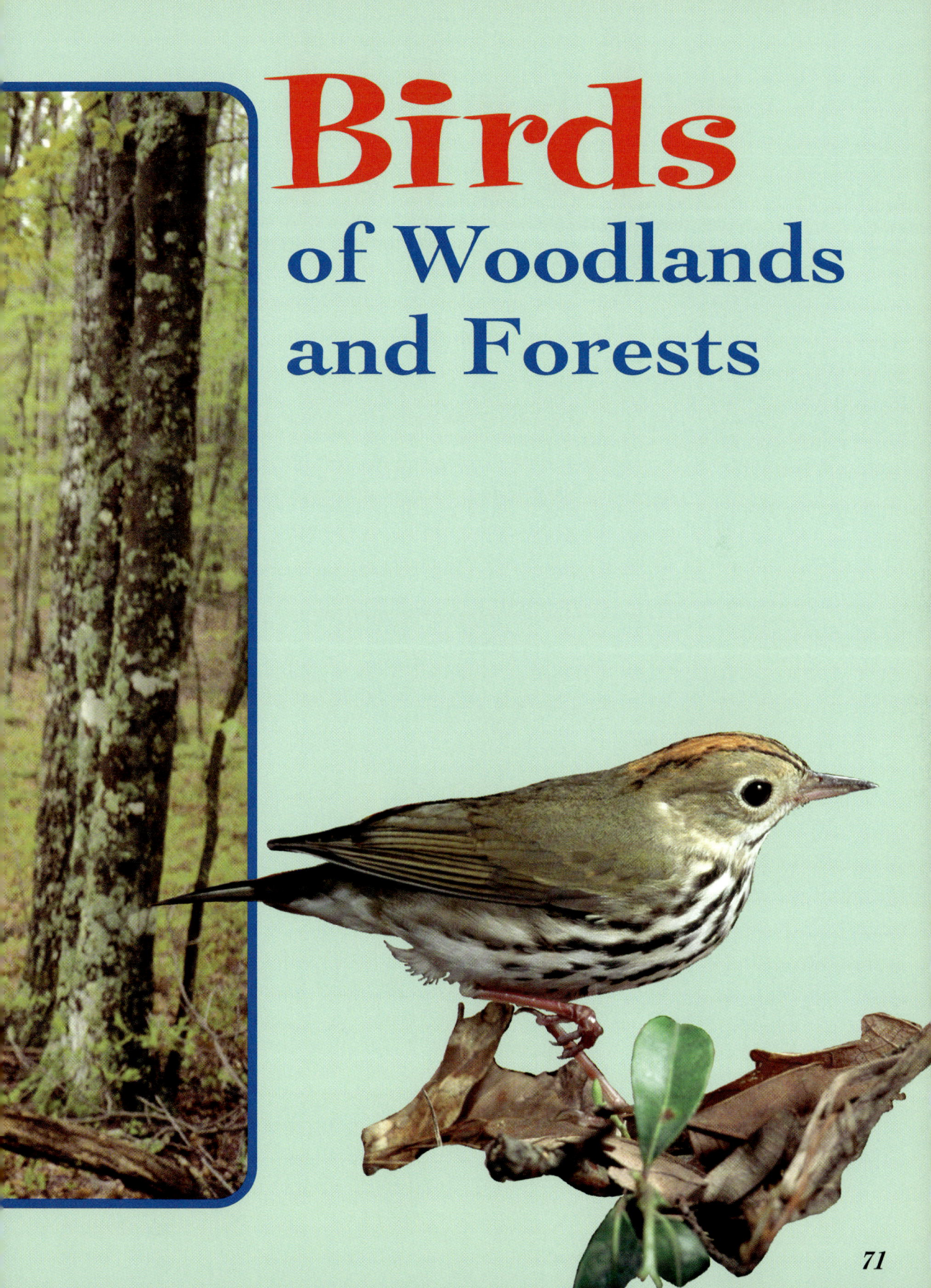

Birds

of Woodlands and Forests

Life in the Woods

It is a chilly March morning in a woods in North America. The sun is just about to rise. On a huge old log stands a bird with handsomely decorated feathers—a male ruffed grouse.

The grouse has claimed as its "territory" the small patch of woods in which the old log lies. If another male should come into this territory, the grouse will fight it! The two birds will peck, kick, and beat each other with their wings. Finally, one bird will give up and run away. The winner will keep the territory.

To the grouse, the old log is the most important part of the territory. The bird stands on the log each sunrise and sunset and does a special task.

Photographs on pages 70—71

A barred owl in a woodland and an ovenbird on the forest floor.

He leans back, pressing his tail against the log. He spreads his wings, like a person stretching. Then he begins to beat the air with his wings, moving them back and forth slowly at first, then speeding up until they move so fast they become a blur. A sound like a rumble of distant thunder fills the air.

Throughout the time of sunrise—and throughout sunset—the grouse frequently beats his wings this way. The booming sound carries far through the woods. The bird makes this noise for the same reason a male robin sings its spring song—to call a female to come be with him and to warn other males to stay out of his territory.

As the gray light of dawn begins to fill the woods, a female grouse hears the booming. At once, she flies straight toward the sound.

The female lands near the log. The male peers at her suspiciously. He hops off the log and walks stiffly toward her. He wiggles his head and hisses. If this newcomer wants a fight, he'll give her one! But the female pays no attention to him. She begins to peck at a tender young dandelion plant. The male realizes she isn't an "invader." He grows calmer. In time, they will mate.

After mating, the female grouse searches until she finds a place to nest. It may be near a stump or fallen log. She chooses a pile of leaves close beside an old stump. She pushes her body into the leaves to make a shallow, scooped-out place. She settles into it. Every other day, she lays a small, pale brown egg, until she has 9 to 12 eggs.

For about the next 24 days, the female sits huddled over the eggs. She leaves the nest only once or twice a day to get food and water. When she comes back, she turns each egg over to make sure that all parts of the egg will get enough warmth.

While the female warms (or *incubates*) her eggs, both she and they are in constant danger. Foxes, raccoons, opossums, skunks, and many other animals that prowl the woods will gladly eat both her and her eggs. Hawks and owls are also her deadly enemies. However, as she sits on the leaves, her body blends into them so well it's almost impossible to see her. A fox may trot by and never even notice the female grouse, because her feathers camouflage (*KAM uh flazh*) her. (Animals that have fur or feathers that help them to blend into their surroundings are using *camouflage*.)

On the 24th day, the female hears noises and feels movement in the eggs beneath her. She begins to walk

nervously around the nest, as the baby birds start to peck their way out of their shells. A few hours later, they are all out. At first, the baby grouse are wet and skinny-looking, with closed eyes. But, quite soon, they are dry and fluffy, with wide, bright eyes.

The odor of the empty eggshells would soon attract the attention of many animals. The mother grouse knows by *instinct* that she must get the young ones away from the nest. (Instinct is a natural way of doing something that animals know, without being taught it.) The mother leads them off to another protected area.

The chicks learn to hide when their mother gives a loud clucking sound that means "danger." They dart for the closest cover and sit low without moving. When everything is quiet again, they scurry out of hiding and join her.

The days pass. They quickly learn to pick up every small moving insect they see. They follow their mother about all day. At night, they all sleep huddled under her wings.

As the young ones grow older, they eat many kinds of plants and occasionally eat insects. After about two weeks, they can fly well enough to reach the low branches of trees. Then they and their mother sleep in a tree each night.

By autumn, the young grouse are just about full grown. There are fewer of them now, for some have

been killed and eaten by other creatures of the woods. Their bodies begin to change.

Grouse store up fat by eating a large amount of wild grapes, berries, and nuts. Immature birds begin to grow a warm downy covering on their bodies and legs. Their toes grow thicker and wider. This makes their feet act as snowshoes to keep the birds from sinking into the snow that will cover the ground through the deep of winter.

Some of these young birds will be "boomers" next spring, beating their wings while standing on an old log. Others will become mothers with families of their own to care for through the spring and summer.

A Bill for Worms

On a moonlit night in a swampy forest, a bird with a long bill walks slowly over a patch of muddy ground.

The bird walks with its head close to the ground. It pauses. Then it pushes its bill down into the soft, damp earth. In the earth, a worm is crawling. The tip of the bird's bill touches it. In an instant, the worm is swallowed!

The long, thin bill of the bird called a woodcock is a marvelous tool for getting the bird's favorite food, earthworms. The woodcock can poke its long bill into

An American woodcock.

soft earth, down to where worms are plentiful. The tip of the bill can be wiggled, like a finger. The woodcock uses it to feel for worms. Even though the bill is deep in the ground, the bird is able to open its bill and swallow the worm.

Woodcocks do their hunting where the ground is soft. So they live mostly in swampy, wet woods, where the ground is moist and muddy. They hunt at night, because that's when earthworms are most active, crawling about near the surface.

During the day, the birds stay hidden in dark places under trees or bushes. Their feathers, which are the color of dead leaves, provide them with camouflage (help them blend into their surroundings so that they're almost invisible). And their eyes are set so far back, they can see in all directions without turning their head.

Woodcocks are good fliers. But they spend a lot of time on the ground and even make their nests on the ground. A woodcock's nest is just a hollow scooped out of the ground—not very deep— and lined with dead leaves. If a mother woodcock feels her babies are in danger, she'll sometimes move them out of the nest.

Shaggy and Whiskered

One of the strangest of all birds lives in some of the moist forests of New Zealand. It has feathery "whiskers" around its bill, its body feathers resemble a shaggy coat of hair, and it has no tail feathers. Its wings are so tiny they are very hard to see, and it cannot fly. It is called a kiwi (*KEE wee*), probably because of the sound the male makes.

In some ways, a kiwi is a lot like another kind of bird that lives in damp woods, the woodcock. Like a woodcock, the kiwi has a long, slim, bendable bill that it pokes into soft earth in search of worms, hunting mostly by night. But, unlike the woodcock, the kiwi has nostrils at the tip of its bill and uses them to sniff out its prey.

A kiwi is between about 18 and 22 inches (45 and 50 centimeters) long. For its size, a female kiwi lays a very large egg. In fact, a 4-pound (1.8-kilogram) kiwi could lay an egg weighing 1 pound (0.45 kilogram)—about one-fourth of her own weight!

At egg-laying time, pairs of male and female kiwis dig winding underground tunnels among the roots of trees or under logs or rocks. The mother kiwi lays her egg in the tunnel. However, it is the male who incubates it. And when the young kiwi is ready to leave the nest, it is the father who takes it out into the world.

A Holiday Bird

Most turkeys that people eat on holidays are raised on farms. But many wild turkeys live in wooded parts of North America. These wild turkeys weigh only about one-third to one-half as much as the domestic, or farm-raised, turkeys. By day, they walk about in search of food—mostly seeds and nuts, but also insects, spiders, grains, and berries. In the evening, they fly up into the tops of trees to spend the night.

A wild turkey.

At mating time, in the spring, male turkeys puff themselves up, spread their feathers, and strut about. They grunt, make a gobble-gobble sound, and shake their feathers to attract females.

After a female turkey mates, she hurries off into the woods to make a nest. She scoops out a hollow under a bush and lays as many as 12 eggs. She incubates the eggs for about a month.

When the baby turkeys hatch, they are able to walk about and look for food right away. Their mother shows them how to search and scratch the ground to find food. In the summer, the females and their young form a large flock and stay together. By the time winter comes, the young have grown. The female and male turkeys may form separate flocks or stay together.

Owls of the Woods

For creatures of the woods, one of the most feared enemies is the owl. A number of kinds of owls live in forests throughout the world, including the great gray owl, the North American barred owl, and the barn owl. All are skillful hunters. They can see well in just the faintest bit of light. They can hear the tiny sounds of a mouse's feet from up to 100 feet (30 meters) away. And they make hardly any noise when they fly.

A great gray owl.

Woodland owls vary in size, from very small (6 inches, or 15 centimeters) to over 2 feet (60 centimeters) long. Depending on their size, they hunt mice, rats, squirrels, rabbits, birds, frogs, worms, and insects. The great horned owl, which also lives in places other than the woodlands, eats opossums, skunks, and even cats. It is a fierce hunter, known as "the tiger of the air!"

Forest owls make their nests and lay their eggs in holes in tree trunks, in hollow stumps, or in old, empty nests of other large birds. Adult owls feed their babies the same things they eat.

The face of a great horned owl.

Flocks of crows will try to drive away any owl they see during the day.

Although woodland owls are night creatures, they can see in daylight. An owl is often "up and around" in the daytime, and this may get it into trouble. Other birds of the woods hate and fear owls. Blue jays and crows, seeing an owl, will set up a tremendous chattering, to warn all other creatures that danger is near. In fact, flocks of jays and crows will actually attack any owl they see, and attempt to drive it away.

The Owl

by Barry Cornwall

In the hollow tree, in the old gray tower,
　　The spectral owl doth dwell;
Dull, hated, despised, in the sunshine hour,
　　But at dusk he's abroad and well!
Not a bird of the forest e'er mates with him;
　　All mock him outright by day;
But at night, when the woods grow still and dim,
　　The boldest will shrink away!
　　　O, when the night falls, and roosts the fowl,
　　　Then, then, is the reign of the hornèd owl!

And the owl hath a bride, who is fond and bold,
　　And loveth the wood's deep gloom;
And, with eyes like the shine of the moonstone cold,
　　She awaiteth her ghastly groom;
Not a feather she moves, not a carol she sings,
　　As she waits in her tree so still;
But when her heart heareth his flapping wings,
　　She hoots out her welcome shrill!
　　　O, when the moon shines, and dogs do howl,
　　　Then, then, is the joy of the hornèd owl!

Mourn not for the owl, nor his gloomy plight!
   The owl hath his share of good:
If a prisoner he be in the broad daylight,
   He is lord in the dark greenwood!
Nor lonely the bird, nor his ghastly mate,
   They are unto each other a pride;
Thrice fonder, perhaps, since a strange, dark fate
   Hath rent them from all beside!
   So, when the night falls, the dogs do howl,
   Sing ho! For the reign of the hornèd owl!
     We know not always
     Who are kings by day,
   But the king of the night is the bold brown owl!

The Mound Builders

Each year, in autumn, a male mallee fowl, sometimes with help from his mate, begins to dig a pit. Scraping and scratching in the Australian scrub, he digs a pit 2 to 3 feet (0.6 to 0.9 meter) deep and 9 feet (2.7 meters) or more wide. He fills this pit with a big pile of dead leaves, twigs, and tree bark. Then he covers the pile with a thick layer of soil or sand, forming a mound 2 to 4 feet (0.6 to 1.2 meters) high. All this work takes several months.

During the next few months, the male will open up the mound every 5 to 10 days so that the mother can lay an egg in it. Each time, he covers up the mound again, so the egg is buried deep inside.

As the sun bakes down, the mound heats up inside, warming the eggs so they can hatch. For the next two to three months, the male visits the mound each day to check its temperature. If it seems to him that the eggs need more heat, he covers the mound with more soil or sand. If it seems the eggs are getting too much heat, he opens up the mound for a time so it can cool.

When the eggs hatch, the young must dig and push their way through

3 feet (0.9 meter) or more of the mound. Sometimes this takes a baby bird as long as 15 hours!

From the moment each baby bird finally breaks through the mound, it is on its own. A baby mallee fowl must quickly learn to look after itself—and it does. It can run soon after it comes out of its mound. It knows how to scratch the ground for seeds and insects to eat. And within several hours it is able to fly up into the low branches of a tree to spend the night.

Mallee fowl of Australia build a big mound in which to lay their eggs.

The Red-headed Forester

From time to time in many a woods in North America there's a sound like someone thumping rapidly on a drum. This sound is made by a pileated (*PY lee AY tihd*) woodpecker. Pileated means "having a pointed cluster of feathers on the head." The woodpecker makes its drumming sound by hammering its bill on a tree limb or trunk.

During the winter, a male pileated woodpecker often hammers to make it known that he's in his territory. As spring approaches, he hammers to attract a mate and to tell other males that this is his territory. The sound carries far through the woods. If a female woodpecker hears the sound, she will fly straight to it.

A pileated woodpecker with young.

But a lot of a pileated woodpecker's hammering is done simply to get food. Ants called carpenter ants make nests in tree trunks, usually in diseased or dead ones. Some kinds of beetles lay their eggs in tree trunks, where they develop into adults. These ants and young beetles are a pileated woodpecker's main food. To get at the creatures, the bird chisels holes with its sharp bill. When it uncovers an insect, it pokes out a long, sticky, spiky tongue and pulls the insect into its mouth.

Pileated woodpeckers also chisel holes in tree trunks to make nests. Inside the hole, the mother woodpecker lays her eggs on a pile of leftover wood chips.

Other **Birds** of Woodlands and Forests

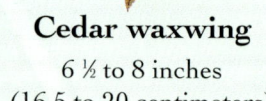

Cedar waxwing
6 ½ to 8 inches
(16.5 to 20 centimeters)

Baltimore oriole
7 to 8 inches
(18 to 20 centimeters)

Tufted titmouse
6 to 6 ½ inches
(15 to 16.5 centimeters)

Scarlet tanager
6 ½ to 7 ½ inches
(16.5 to 19 centimeters)

Red-eyed vireo
5 ½ to 6 ½ inches
(14 to 16.5 centimeters)

Ruby-crowned kinglet
3 ½ to 4 ½ inches
(9 to 11 centimeters)

White-breasted nuthatch
5 to 6 inches
(13 to 15 centimeters)

Birds
of Lakes,
Rivers, and
Swamps

A Watery Way of Life

On a small lake in North America, a male horned grebe *(greeb)* is seeking a mate. He swims about, singing his love song—loud croaks, chattering sounds, and shrieks! His noisy song echoes across the bright waters of the lake.

After a time, the male meets a female that seems interested in him. He begins a "dance" to attract her, and she joins him.

They face each other, then swim around in a circle. They nod and turn their heads to show off their "horns," the streaks of golden feathers on each side of the head. Then they suddenly dive out of sight.

Photographs on pages 94—95

Swans at a swannery (a place where these birds are bred) in Abbotsbury, England, and a green-backed heron.

Moments later, the birds pop up again—carrying clumps of water plants in their bills—and they bow to each other. Then they rush across the water together, splashing as they go. Soon, the two birds mate.

A short time later, nest-building begins. Grebes spend all their lives in the water. They are not well adapted to being on land—they have very poor balance when they walk—so they need a nest they can swim to. The nest they build is like a raft, floating on the water.

The two grebes pick a shallow part of the lake, where reeds and cattails are sticking up out of the water. The birds dive and bring up billful after billful of dead plants from the lake bottom. Working quickly, they pile the soggy, muddy plants together to make a large mound. The mound may be fastened to the stalk of a cattail or some other water plant.

When the nest is almost finished, the female grebe climbs on top of it. She wiggles her body, forming a shallow cup in the top of the nest. She then squats down in the cup. In time, she lays five eggs. During the time in which the eggs are laid and *incubated* (warmed so that they will hatch), the grebes continue to work on the nest, which may grow to a width of 1 foot (30 centimeters). The male and female will take turns incubating the eggs.

The eggs hatch in about 25 days. The baby birds are covered with tiny, soft, dark gray feathers—called *down*—which are striped and spotted with white.

As soon as the baby grebes are dry, they take to the water. They can swim and dive right away. However, they spend most of their time riding on their parents' backs. Even when the mother and father grebe dive for food, the little ones stay aboard.

The baby grebes soon begin to dart after insects, tadpoles, small frogs, and tiny fish. As the young grebes become more and more able to care for themselves, the male grebe goes away, usually taking two of the young birds with him. The mother grebe stays with the other three young birds. The young stay with each parent until they are fully grown.

By autumn, the grebes on the little lake no longer have the golden streaks on each side of the head. These feathers are just for the mating season. But now it is time for *migration*—that is, the time when such birds as grebes move to a different area to find more food or a better climate.

One by one, the grebes depart. They take off by running a long way along the surface of the water, flapping their wings until they finally get into the air. Grebes are good fliers, but it isn't easy for them to take off, so they fly only when they must.

Horned grebes live in North America and in northern Europe and Asia. In Europe, they are known as Slavonian grebes. There are a number of different kinds of grebes but all are water birds.

Longlegs

A flamingo looks like a bird that someone made up! Its long, skinny, legs look as if they might break under the bird's weight. Its long, thin neck can twist and turn in ways that you could never imitate!

But a flamingo's long legs and long neck are important to its way of life. A flamingo wades through the shallow water of a lake or lagoon to find its food. Its legs keep its body up out of the water. Its neck allows it to reach down into the water to get its food.

When it wants to eat, a flamingo holds its head upside down in the water—with the top of its head pointing downward. The bird then opens its mouth to let water in and closes its mouth, squeezing the water out with its tongue. Each time the flamingo does this, tiny plants and animals in the water are trapped by small "strainers" inside the bird's mouth. The bird then swallows the trapped food.

Flamingo nests are mounds of mud that stick up out of shallow water. The flamingos make these nests by heaping up mud that they scrape off the lake bottom. At the top of the mound, the female scoops a shallow pit. In this, she lays one egg.

The female and her mate take turns incubating the egg for about a month, until it hatches. The baby flamingo is fed a sort of milky liquid that both parents make in their throats, called *crop milk*.

Enormous flocks of flamingos are found in lakes and lagoons in Africa, southern Asia, Europe, South

America, and the Caribbean. There are at least four different kinds of flamingos. The largest kind, called the greater flamingo, is about 5 feet (1.5 meters) tall. The smallest kind, the lesser flamingo, is about 40 inches (1 meter) tall.

Lesser flamingos in Kenya.

Waterfowl

Ducks, geese, and swans are related. They are all known as waterfowl, because they spend most of their lives in lakes, ponds, and rivers, and along seacoasts. They all have webbed feet and rather short legs. They are fine swimmers. The oil on their feathers makes the feathers waterproof.

Swans are the giants of the waterfowl group. They are large birds, with long, graceful necks. Some swans can stretch their necks to reach as high as a person's chest. Geese are smaller than swans, and they have shorter necks. Ducks are the smallest of all, and they have the shortest necks.

You have probably heard or read that geese honk and ducks quack. That isn't quite true. Although geese do honk, they can make other sounds, too. Some geese

A male mandarin duck.

cackle, much like a hen. Others yap or gurgle. And while many ducks do quack, many can also make whistling noises. Wood ducks can squeal, squeak, and cluck. And a male redhead duck meows like a cat!

Swans can also make several kinds of noises. One of the calls that a trumpeter swan makes sounds like a trumpet or bugle. When a type of swan called a mute swan calls to its mate, it makes a snorting sound.

Different kinds of waterfowl eat different things and have different ways of getting their food. Some kinds of ducks, such as mallards, pintails, and teals, are known as "dabbling" or "dipping" ducks. To get their food—which is mainly water plants and seeds—these ducks actually "duck" their heads underwater, with their feet and tails sticking straight up in the air. Swans also feed in this way.

Canvasbacks, redheads, and several other kinds of ducks are known as diving ducks. These birds dive and eat underwater. Their food is mostly roots, seeds, insects, and snails. However, there are some kinds of diving ducks that feed in the sea and eat mostly shellfish or fish.

Most kinds of geese are able to get much of their food on land. They eat mainly grasses and other plants. Their bills can clip off the tops of plants as neatly as if someone had cut them off with a scissors.

Waterfowl have several different ways of making nests. Swans make big, bulky piles of grass and

Mute swans.

water plants close to water. Both the male and female swans work to make the nest. Some goose nests are like swan nests. Some kinds of geese make their nests in shrubs or low trees, or in spaces in cliffs.

Most dabbling ducks nest on the ground. But the ducks known as perching ducks, which perch in trees, build nests in the holes in trees. And shelducks make their nests in rabbit holes and other animal *burrows* (holes an animal digs for a home or a hiding place).

Before nest-building time, special feathers begin to grow on the breasts of female waterfowl. These very soft feathers are called nest-down. After the female has laid her eggs, she plucks these feathers with her bill and lines her nest with them. For hundreds of years, people have collected nest-down feathers, especially from eider ducks. They use the down to fill pillows, comforters, and coats.

Baby waterfowl hatch with their eyes open and with down on their bodies. They can walk and swim soon after hatching. While the baby birds are growing up, first one parent and then the other *molts* (sheds) all of

Snow geese.

its long wing and tail feathers. During this time, the parent cannot fly. It stays hidden in tall weeds. By the end of summer, when the young ones are able to fly, both parents have new flight feathers. In fall, all the birds can migrate together.

When many kinds of waterfowl migrate, they fly in a *flock* (a group of birds of one type that feed, live, or travel together). The flock forms patterns as it flies. For example, most waterfowl, including Canada geese, fly in a pattern shaped like a *V*. Some waterfowl, such as the geese known as black brants, may fly in a single, slanting line, with one bird behind another. In this way, the leader, pushing through the air first, makes a "path" for the others. As one leader gets tired, another bird moves up to take its place.

Male, female, and baby waterfowl all have special names. A male duck is a drake, a female is a duck, and the young one is a duckling. A male goose is a gander, a female is a goose, and a baby goose is a gosling. A male swan is a cob, a female is a pen, and a baby swan is a cygnet *(SIHG niht)*. A group of ducks or swans is called a flock, but a group of geese is often called a gaggle!

Duck's Ditty
by Kenneth Grahame

All along the backwater,
Through a rushes tall,
Ducks are a-dabbling,
Up tails all!

Ducks' tails, drakes' tails,
Yellow feet a-quiver,
Yellow bills all out of sight
Busy in the river!

Slushy green undergrowth
Where the roaches[1] swim —
Here we keep our larder,[2]
Cool and full and dim.

Everyone for what he likes!
We like to be
Heads down, tails up,
Dabbling free!

High in the blue above
Swifts whirl and call —
We are down a-dabbling
Up tails all!

1. a kind of fish
2. food supply

The Snail Snatcher

It is early morning in a swamp in Florida. A brown bird with long legs and a white-speckled neck and back stands on a mudbank. It stands on one leg, with the other tucked up under its body. After a time, it puts this leg down and walks along the mudbank, toward the water. It seems to limp as it walks. This odd way of walking has given the bird its name—limpkin.

The limpkin wades into the shallow water. It moves along with its body just above the surface.

Stretching its long neck down into the water, it feels the muddy bottom with its long bill. After a time, it finds what it is looking for—a large snail crawling in the mud. Using the tip of its bill like a pair of tweezers, the limpkin picks up the snail and wades back to shore.

The snail is hiding inside its shell, of course, with the "door" tightly closed. But the limpkin wedges the shell into a crack in a tree to hold it firmly. The bird then waits. Before long, the snail feels safe enough to start coming out of the shell.

Jab! The limpkin's bill stabs down. With a jerk of its head, the bird yanks the snail all the way out of the shell. It holds the snail in its bill for a while. Then, down goes the snail with a big gulp!

Limpkins live in swamps and marshes in Florida, the Caribbean, Mexico, and Central and South America. They can swim well and can fly, but they seldom do either. They usually wade in the water, searching for food, and they also *perch* (sit) among the branches of trees.

A limpkin nest is a loose pile of twigs, leaves, and other bits of dead plants. Some limpkins put their nests in bushes or trees, but others build nests in clumps of grass on the ground. A female limpkin lays about six eggs. She and her mate take turns incubating the eggs and caring for the young. 🖋

Lily-Trotters

The warm, blue water of the Mexican marsh is very still. Hundreds of lily pads float lightly on the surface. But the lily pads are hopping with activity! Small, long-legged northern jacanas *(zhah sun NAHZ)*, or lily-trotters, are running daintily on top of the leaves.

Jacanas live in warm, watery places all over the world. They are usually found on plants that float on the water's surface. Jacanas jab their bills into the marsh to pick up water insects and seeds. The birds hide and stay perfectly still when danger is near. They swim or fly away when the danger approaches.

Female jacanas search for the males they want to mate with. After a female lays eggs, the male incubates them and later rears the baby jacanas. Soon after birth, the young birds follow their fathers around the marsh.

Belted kingfisher.

Expert Fisher

A belted kingfisher sits on a tree branch watching the clear forest stream below. Suddenly, it swoops down over the water, dives in, and spears a fish. The bird shoots back up to its perch and bangs the fish's head on the branch. Then the bird flips the fish into the air and swallows it headfirst.

Belted kingfishers are excellent hunters that live mostly by themselves. They usually hunt for fish in lakes and streams throughout North America. Other kingfishers, such as the Australian kookaburra *(KUK uh BUR uh)*, eat frogs, snakes, mice, worms, and insects.

In spring, belted kingfishers get together to mate and rear their young. They dig a long tunnel ending in a large, round area where the female may lay five to seven eggs. The male and female take turns incubating the eggs.

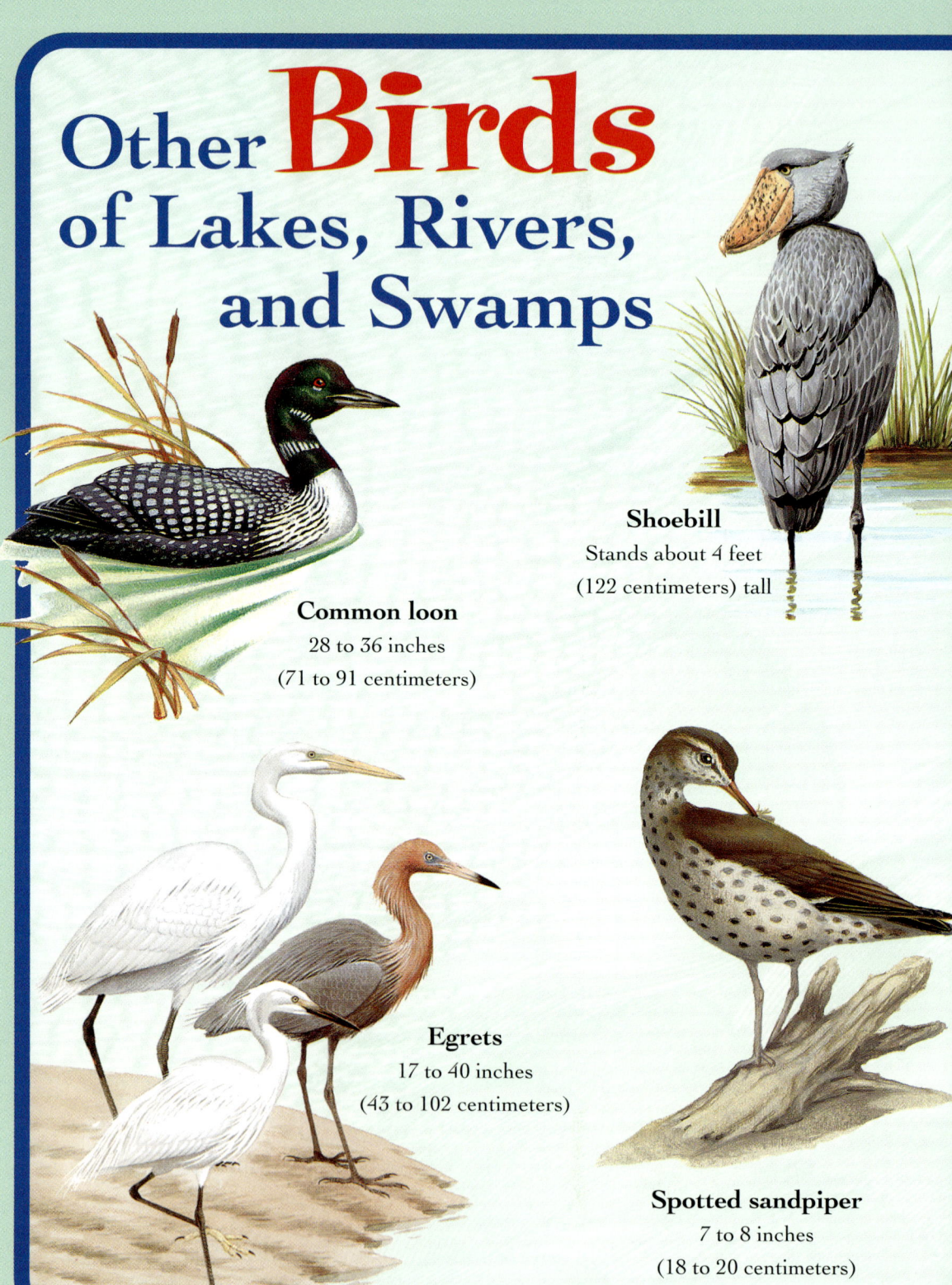

Other **Birds**
of Lakes, Rivers, and Swamps

Shoebill
Stands about 4 feet
(122 centimeters) tall

Common loon
28 to 36 inches
(71 to 91 centimeters)

Egrets
17 to 40 inches
(43 to 102 centimeters)

Spotted sandpiper
7 to 8 inches
(18 to 20 centimeters)

California gull
20 to 23 inches
(51 to 58 centimeters)

Great blue heron
Stands about 4 feet
(122 centimeters) tall

Louisiana water thrush
About 6 ¼ inches
(16 centimeters)

Birds
of the
Mountains

The Giant Glider

High above a mountainous part of southern California, a bird glides on outstretched wings. It is a very large bird, with a body about 4 feet (1.2 meters) long. Its wings stretch about 10 feet (3 meters) from tip to tip. This amazing creature is one of the largest of all flying birds—a California condor.

The condor isn't a very pretty bird. Its body and wings are solid black, except for a snowy-white strip on the underside of each wing. It has no feathers on its wrinkled, reddish-orange head and neck. Its eyes are bright red, and its ears are just holes surrounded by lumpy swirls of skin.

However, the flight of the condor is very graceful and beautiful. It soars and glides in vast, sweeping circles. It knows how to ride the currents of warm air, called *thermals*, that rise from the ground, so that the condor hardly ever has to flap its wings. The condor simply lets the air currents carry it along for miles.

Photographs on pages 114—115

A bald eagle in flight and a Steller's jay.

As the condor soars, it turns its wrinkled head from side to side, peering down at the open land spread out below. It is seeking food. The condor is a flesh-eater, but it does not kill other creatures for its meals. Instead, it looks for an animal that is already dead, called *carrion*. This is why the condor flies in wide circles so high in the sky—so that it has a better chance of seeing a dead animal on the ground below.

Although it may fly great distances each day in its search for food, a condor isn't always able to find something to eat. It must sometimes go for days without eating. But the bird we're watching is in luck. It spies a large, brown form lying in a brushy canyon—a deer that was injured and died.

The condor thrives on such large animals as deer, sheep, and cows. These animals have so much meat that the condor can eat about 2 pounds (0.9 kilogram) of it at one time. However, the bird may also eat smaller creatures, such as dead squirrels and rabbits. Condors do not care for the meat of any creature that has been dead for too long. They prefer fresh meat.

The condor descends cautiously, in broad, slow circles. Finally it lands, coming to a rather clumsy, running stop. A cluster of ravens pecking at the deer's body quickly fly away as the condor approaches. The ravens have no wish to argue with this giant bird!

The condor paces forward in stately fashion, much like a strutting turkey. Bending down, it starts to peck

at the deer's body with its strong,
sharp beak.

Watching with keen eyes as they soared
high up, other condors noticed the first condor
glide down. This told them food had been found.
Soon, several of the big birds surround the
deer. They share peaceably, with only an occasional
squabble breaking out when two birds happen to want
the same piece of food.

In time, the first condor has eaten its fill. Turning away,
the bird leans forward and rubs its head and neck on the
grass to clean itself. The condor's bald head and neck are
well suited to its way of life. To get its fill, the condor
often has to push its head down into the bloody inside of

a dead animal. Feathers on its head and neck would get
dirty and bloody, but its bare skin is easy to clean.

Many people dislike condors and other birds that
eat dead creatures. But these birds do a very useful
and important job. They begin the work of disposing
of a dead animal by opening up its
body. Then other creatures—including
insects and very tiny organisms—do

their part to finish breaking down the remains of the dead animal. So, one dead animal can nourish many living things.

The condor finishes cleaning itself and decides to take to the air again. It runs along clumsily, hopping and flapping its wings, before it finally rises into the air. Then its clumsiness vanishes. It becomes a graceful glider soaring on the breeze.

Looking at a California condor is like looking millions of years into the past! Fossils show that birds very much like the California condor lived long ago, along with various animals that have since become *extinct*. (A species, or type, of animal becomes extinct when every one of its kind has died.) The condor is a link to the prehistoric world.

California condors are rare. Their numbers declined in past years for several reasons, including the destruction of their *habitat* (a place or area where an animal or plant naturally lives and grows), poisoning, and even egg collecting. A condor lays only one egg every two years, so if that egg is lost, the condor population may be seriously affected. Conservationists are working to protect condors and to increase their population, using such methods as raising birds in *captivity* (protected places not in the wild). In the early 2000's, there were more than 130 condors in captivity and more than 80 in the wild, and these numbers were slowly increasing.

A golden eagle.

The King of Birds

Eagles are among the swiftest, most powerful, and most graceful of birds. They soar freely over huge *territories* (areas an animal chooses for a place to live) that may spread across 60 square miles (160 square kilometers). They circle as high as 300 feet (90 meters) in the air above their *prey* (an animal that is caught and eaten by another animal). Then they fold their wings back and dive. At the last minute, they snap their wings open and grab their prey in razor-sharp talons.

Eagles nest high in treetops or on the top of cliffs. They often stay with the same mate and use the same nest year after year. Female eagles usually lay one, two, or three spotted eggs. After the eggs hatch, both of the parents care for and feed the young for about three months.

There are several kinds of eagles, and they eat different things. Golden eagles eat all types of small mammals and birds—and sometimes even a young deer or lamb. Certain eagles, such as the harpy eagle and the Philippine eagle, eat monkeys and other mammals. Bald eagles and many other eagles eat both mammals and fish.

Bald eagle with prey.

The Eagle
By Alfred, Lord Tennyson

He clasps the crag with crooked hands;
Close to the sun in lonely lands,
Ringed with the azure world, he stands.

The wrinkled sea beneath him crawls;
He watches from his mountain walls,
And like a thunderbolt, he falls.

The Bone Eater

If you were thinking about an animal that eats bones, you might be thinking of a dog. But there are certain types of birds that also eat bones. One type lives in the mountains of Africa, southern Europe, and central Asia. It is the lammergeier *(LAM uhr GY uhr)*, or bearded vulture.

The lammergeier is a large bird. Its body is nearly 4 feet (1.2 meters) long. Its wings stretch between 9 and 10 feet (2.7 and 3 meters) from one wing tip to the other. It soars over the mountain peaks and valleys, peering down in search of the bodies of dead creatures. Sometimes it waits patiently while other vultures eat the flesh of a dead sheep or some other animal. When these other birds leave, the lammergeier goes down to eat the remains.

The lammergeier eats a lot of meat. It can also swallow small bones whole. It takes large bones in its beak and, flying high into the air, drops them so that the bones shatter on the rocks below. Then it flies down and chews on the *marrow*, the soft part that is found inside the bones.

Lammergeiers build huge nests inside caves or on cliff ledges. The nests are made of tree branches, bones, and animal fur and skins.

A Hunter in the Sky

Like the eagle, the peregrine *(PEHR uh grihn)* falcon is a hunter. Instead of hunting animals that live on the ground, however, it catches other birds in midair.

A peregrine falcon is a fast flier. It can chase and catch most small birds. To catch larger birds, it dives from a great height at speeds of up to 200 miles (320 kilometers) an hour! It strikes with its clawed toes. Then it bites into the neck, killing its prey at once.

Peregrine falcons are found worldwide in different habitats, including frozen tundra, sea coasts, and high mountains. These birds usually make their nests on the edges of cliffs. Sometimes they even nest in cities on the ledges of skyscrapers!

By the 1960's, pesticide poisoning nearly wiped out peregrine falcons in the United States. However, conservation efforts, including breeding the birds in captivity and cutting back on pesticide use, have brought back the peregrine falcon.

A peregrine falcon.

An Underwater Hunter

On a rock in the middle of a clear, cold mountain stream, an American dipper flicks its tail and then dives to the bottom of the stream. When it spies its prey, the bird quickly snaps up the prey in its bill.

American dippers get most of their food underwater. They eat small fish. They may also eat insects, including the *larvae* (young) of stone flies and mayflies.

Dippers are *perching birds*—that is, birds that belong to an *order* (scientific grouping) that is known as Passeriformes. These birds share a similar type of foot, which allows them to grasp tightly onto a perch. But dippers are also especially suited to living in and around the water. Their feathers are waterproof. The birds also have an extra, *transparent* (see-through) eyelid, so they can actually see with their eyes closed underwater! And they have a special flap to keep water out of their nostrils. So dippers can live even in rapidly rushing streams.

Other Birds
of the Mountains

Mountain bluebird
7 ¼ inches
(18 centimeters)

Kea
15 to 20 inches
(38 to 51 centimeters)

Andean condor
About 52 inches
(132 centimeters)

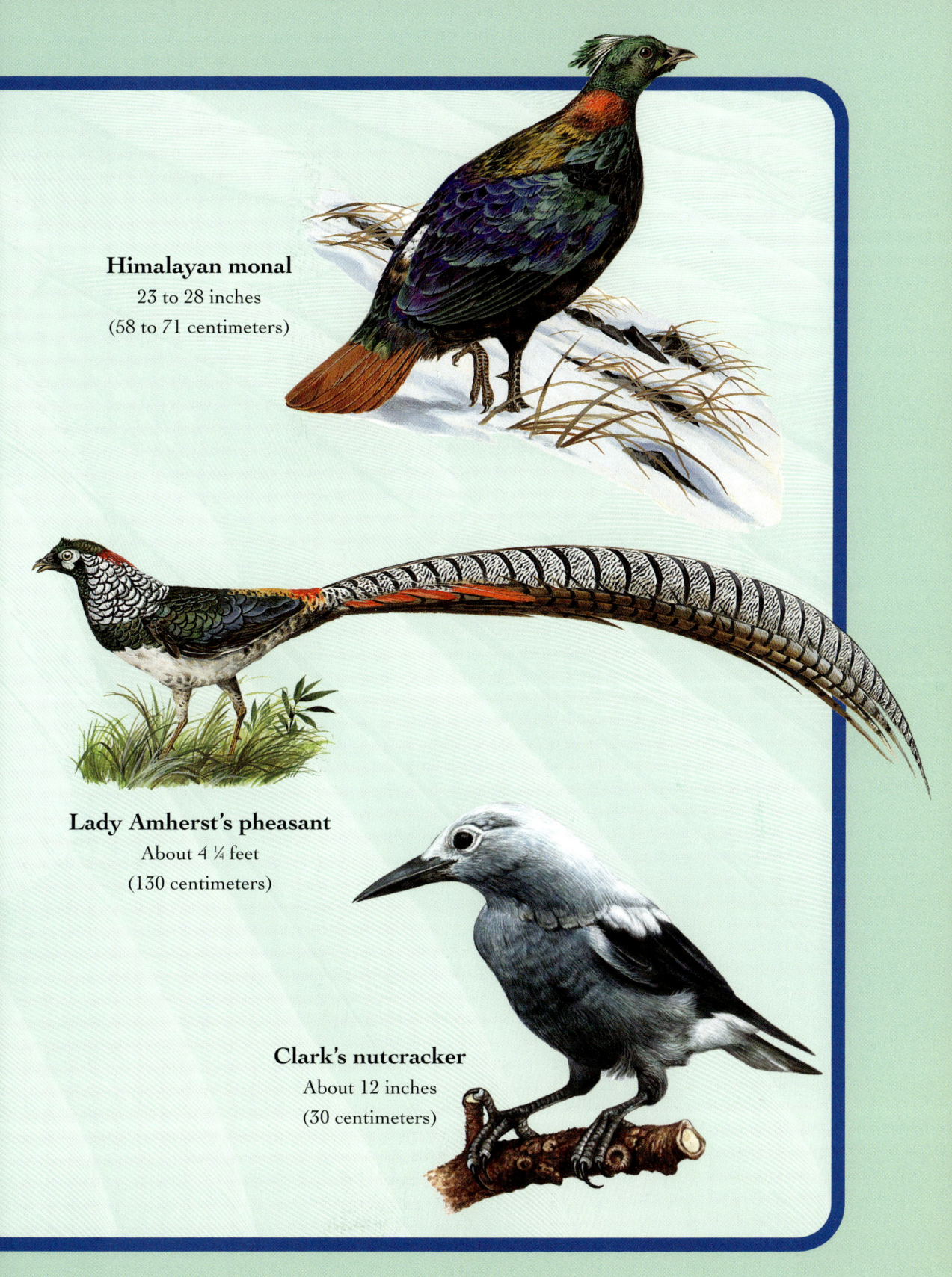

Himalayan monal
23 to 28 inches
(58 to 71 centimeters)

Lady Amherst's pheasant
About 4 ¼ feet
(130 centimeters)

Clark's nutcracker
About 12 inches
(30 centimeters)

Birds
of the
Rain Forest

Artistic Birds

In a dense forest in Australia, a bird was hard at work. It had already made a thick "carpet" of woven twigs on the ground. Now, using its bill, it jammed other twigs into the carpet to make a long wall. Then the bird built another wall of twigs across from the first. The two walls enclosed a narrow path just wide enough for the bird to walk through.

The bird flew off. It was back shortly, with some charcoal in its bill. It chewed the charcoal into a black paste. Then it picked up a piece of bark in its bill. Using the bark like a sponge, the bird swabbed the black "paint" on the insides of the walls of twigs!

Photographs on pages 130—131

Two scarlet macaws in Peru and a blue-winged mountain tanager in Venezuela.

When this decorating was done, the bird flew off again. It returned carrying a blue flower. The bird placed the flower on the carpet of twigs. Then it stepped back with its head cocked to one side.

After a moment, the bird stepped forward and moved the flower. Then it flew off again. Some time later, the bird returned. This time, it had the shiny blue wing of a beetle in its bill. This too, it placed on the carpet of twigs.

The bird went back and forth like this for the rest of the day. Each time it returned, it brought a new decoration—a berry, another flower, a bird feather, and even the plastic cover of a ballpoint pen. Most of these things were blue, but one was yellow. Finally, the bird was finished with its decorating. It flew up into a nearby tree and began to sing.

A structure made of leafy branches is called a *bower*. A bird that makes such a structure is the bowerbird. Male bowerbirds make beautiful bowers to attract female bowerbirds at mating time. When a female bird comes to see the bower, the male steps inside and performs. He stretches his neck, opens his wings, spreads out his tail, and sings. If the female is charmed with this display, she becomes his mate!

Different kinds of bowerbirds make different kinds of bowers, such as large domes, pyramids, tunnels, or arches. All of these birds decorate their bowers with such natural items as snail shells, glittery beetle wings,

colorful berries, flowers, and stones. They may even
use bits of glass, paper, cloth, bottle caps, and other
things that people have left lying about. In addition to the
satin bowerbird, several other kinds of bowerbirds
"paint" their bowers.

Bowerbirds live in Australia and on the nearby island
of New Guinea. They eat mainly fruit, but they may also
eat flowers, insects, and worms. Some of the bowers that

these birds make are so fancy that it's hard to imagine animals making them. The first explorers to see a bowerbird's work thought the bower had been built by people.

A bowerbird with items for its nest.

Hidden in Plain Sight

The potoo *(poh TOO)*, which lives in the tropics, can't fly fast or dive deep or hunt especially well. But it has a different talent. It knows how to hide in plain sight. An adult potoo spends its days sitting completely still on a branch or stump. With its bill thrust into the air, it looks like part of the branch. The bird leaves its *perch* (the place where it sits and rests) to hunt for insects only after night falls.

Potoos don't build nests. A female lays a single egg in the hollow of a broken branch or in a *snag* (a tree or branch held in a river or lake). This way, the birds can hide both themselves and their eggs. Once hatched, baby potoos are expert hiders, just like their parents. They sit still in their hollows. They are covered in pale tan *down* (fine, soft feathers) and look more like fungus than like birds—and that keeps them safe from harm.

A female potoo lays her egg on the top of a broken branch.

A potoo in a tree branch.

Big, Bright Bills

Toucans are famous for their big, bright bills. There are about 40 different kinds of toucans, and they all have large, long, brightly colored bills. Some toucans have a bill nearly as long as their body. Although these bills look heavy, they aren't. The inside of the bill is like a honeycomb, with many hollow places. The outside is a thin, tough shell that provides strength. The bill's edges are sharp and jagged, like a saw.

Most birds' bills are special tools that help the birds get certain kinds of food. A toucan might be able to get its favorite foods—berries and other small fruits, insects, and spiders—with a smaller bill. Sometimes, however, toucans also eat larger creatures, such as snakes and small birds and mammals. For this food, toucans need their big, sawlike bills for "chewing."

Toucans live in warm, wet forests, from Mexico to Peru, Brazil, and northeastern Argentina. Some toucans live by themselves, but others form *flocks* (groups of birds of one type that feed, live, or travel together) of up to about 20 birds. The birds often hop about in the top branches of the trees, plucking berries and other food with the tips of their bills. They may also snap up baby birds from their nests.

Toucans are playful creatures. They like to play catch with their food. With its bill, one bird may toss a berry into the air, and another will catch it. Some toucans also have "duels," in which they playfully use their bills like swords!

Cave Birds

Imagine the inside of a large cave in a South American rain forest. Inside this cave it is pitch-black. In the blackness, there is constant noise — screeches, wails, and clicking sounds. Up near the roof of the cave, many creatures are flying. They turn and wheel swiftly in the darkness. Never once do they bump into one another, or into the rocky walls or ceiling.

What are these creatures? Bats live in caves and can fly in darkness without bumping into anything. Are these creatures bats? No, they are oilbirds — birds that are a little like bats in a way. Like bats, these birds have a kind of sonar *(SOH nahr)* system in their bodies. Sonar allows animals to use sounds to "see" their way in darkness.

As an oilbird flies about in the cave, it makes clicking noises. The sound waves that make up these

noises shoot out ahead of the bird. If the sound waves
strike something, they come bouncing back. The bird's
ears pick up these returning sounds. From these
echoes, the bird can tell that something is ahead of it.
It can even tell how big the thing is, and how far away
it is! This is how the oilbird can fly through the cave
without bumping into things.

By day, oilbirds rest on rocks or ledges in their cave.
At night, they fly out into the forest to feed. Outside
the cave, they don't need their sonar system. Like owls,
they can see in darkness as long as there is some
moonlight or starlight. All night, the oilbirds hover
among the trees, plucking palm-tree fruits and eating
them as they fly. Before morning, they go streaming
back into their dark caves.

These birds are called oilbirds because they have a
lot of oil in their bodies. Baby oilbirds are fed the same
rich, oily palm fruits their parents eat. So they grow
very, very plump—eventually weighing more than the
older birds. They lose this extra weight before they
begin flying.

Jungle Runner

Cassowaries *(KAS uh wehr eez)* live in forests in northern Australia and New Guinea and on nearby islands. There are three kinds of cassowaries. The biggest cassowary is about 5 feet (1.5 meters) tall and weighs as much as 120 pounds (54 kilograms). Cassowaries can't fly, but they can run as fast as 30 miles (48 kilometers) an hour. And they can jump as high as 5 feet (1.5 meters) in the air.

Cassowaries eat mostly berries and other fruits, but they may also eat other parts of plants, as well as insects and small mammals. Cassowaries often live in pairs, made up of a male and female. When they nest, cassowaries make a big untidy pile of leaves and sticks at the foot of a tree. The female lays from three to eight blotchy green eggs, and the male *incubates* the eggs (keeps them warm until they hatch). Then he cares for the young birds until they can look after themselves.

Cassowaries.

142

True Dazzlers

In the forests of New Guinea live some of the most beautiful of all birds. When explorers first brought some of these birds' feathers to Europe, they also brought with them the idea that the birds came from paradise, or heaven. Because of this, the birds became known as birds-of-paradise.

There are about 40 different *species* (kinds) of birds-of-paradise. Most are very colorful. At mating time, the males show off their bright colors and fancy feathers to attract females. They strut, dance, and spread their feathers. Often, many male birds-of-paradise of the same species perform at the same time from nearby perches in the treetops. Females watch these performances and choose the bird they like best.

A male bird-of-paradise (left) displaying to a female.

Blue bird-of-paradise
As part of its mating dance, this bird hangs upside down.

Wilson's bird-of-paradise

King of Saxony
bird-of-paradise

Six-wired
bird-of-paradise

145

Terror of the Treetops

The harpy eagle is the terror of the treetops in the forests of much of South America! Weighing more than 10 pounds (4.5 kilograms) and standing 3 feet (91 centimeters) tall, it is one of the largest of all eagles. The wingspan of the harpy eagle reaches 7 feet (2 meters).

This bird hunts monkeys, sloths, and other large tree-dwelling animals. At times, it may dive down to the forest floor to seize an agouti *(uh GOO tee)*, a small, ratlike animal that lives in forests.

Harpy eagles are fast fliers. They usually speed through a forest in short spurts, stopping to perch on trees to look and listen for *prey* (an animal that is caught and eaten by another animal). A harpy eagle seizes its prey with a killing grip of its clawed feet.

Most of the time, a harpy eagle lives by itself. But at mating season, pairs of these eagles get together and build large stick nests high in the tops of tall trees. Mating pairs only breed every other year — after mating the female lays one to two eggs. When the eggs hatch, both the male and female eagles go hunting food for their young ones.

Harpy eagles are named for the "flying monsters" called *harpies* in ancient Greek and Roman mythology. Harpies were said to be fierce, savage beings with the head of a woman and the wings, legs, and body of a bird of prey.

"Jailbirds"

When a female trumpeter hornbill is ready to lay eggs, she puts herself in "jail!"

At egg-laying time, a female hornbill looks for a tree with a hole in it—like a little cave. Then she goes inside the hole. With the help of her mate, who stays on the outside of the hole, she builds a wall across the hole's entrance. The wall is made mostly of mud. The nest is always made during a rainy time, so there is plenty of mud around.

While the male hornbill brings billfulls of mud, the female builds the wall. She works from inside the hole, so that slowly she walls herself in. Finally, the entrance is completely covered, except for a narrow slit in the middle. The mud dries hard as rock, and there's the female hornbill—in "jail!"

Once the hornbill walls herself in, she and her baby hornbills are safe from snakes, monkeys, and other creatures. Of course, she and her young have to eat, and that's why the narrow slit was left in the wall. The male hornbill brings fruit or insects and feeds them to his family through the hole. He spends most of his time bringing food to the walled-up nest.

When the young are about half grown, the mother hornbill breaks out of her jail by battering down the wall with her bill. However, as soon as she is out, the small hornbills start to rebuild the wall! They, too, leave a narrow slit through which their parents can feed them. The young hornbills remain "jailbirds" until

*Trumpeter
hornbill.*

they are ready to fly. Then they and their parents break
down the wall again.

There are a number of different kinds of hornbills.
They generally live in flocks in the hot forests of Africa
and parts of Asia. Some hornbills are no more than 12
inches (30 centimeters) long. Others are nearly as big
as a turkey.

Chatterboxes

Parrots are birds that are well known for their ability to "talk." They also can imitate many other sounds, including whistles and squeaking doors. Although pet parrots can be trained to repeat certain words, wild parrots usually don't say words. This is because they don't live among people, so they never hear any words. But wild parrots do often imitate the sounds of nature, such as the calls of other animals. They also do a lot of screeching and squawking.

A blue-fronted parrot (above) and an African gray parrot (below).

Wild parrots spend most of their time in trees. They usually nest in holes in trees or rocks. And they like to eat fruit, nuts, and seeds from trees. Parrots are

A lorikeet.

good climbers. They use their feet and bills to pull themselves up and around in the trees where they live.

Many different kinds of parrots, including the large *macaws (muh KAWZ)*, live in South American forests. Other members of the parrot family live in Africa, Australia, and Asia. Many of these birds are brightly colored—and this helps protect them. Sitting high up in the branches of trees, brightly colored parrots can look like leaves, flowers, or pieces of fruit!

Other **Birds**
of the Rain Forest

Blue-diademed motmot

15 to 16 inches

(38 to 41 centimeters)

Resplendent quetzal

35 to 38 inches

(89 to 97 centimeters)

White-necked jacobin

About 4 ½ inches

(11.5 centimeters)

Hoatzin

About 24 inches

(61 centimeters)

Paradise tanager
About 5 ½ inches
(14 centimeters)

Scarlet macaw
About 35 inches
(89 centimeters)

Red junglefowl
Up to 26 to 28 inches
(66 to 71 centimeters)

Yellow-headed parrot
About 14 inches
(35 centimeters)

Birds
of the Desert

The Speedy Snake Killer

The rattlesnake was ready to strike! It had its head lifted and drawn back. Its jaws were stretched wide open. The snake glared at the large and awkward-looking bird that faced it. The rattler was young and small, but its bite would easily kill the bird. And the snake could strike in the blink of an eye.

The bird, however, seemed unafraid. It circled the snake swiftly, forcing the snake to swing around to follow it. Suddenly, the bird made a lightning-fast lunge at the snake. At once, the snake struck!

Photographs on pages 154—155

A Gambel's quail and a cactus wren.

But—the bird was not there. The lunge was a trick. At the last instant, the bird dodged. The snake missed its strike and fell full-length on the ground. In a flash, the bird darted in. With its long, pointed bill, the bird stabbed the snake's head and hammered the reptile against the ground. Then the bird calmly picked the snake up in its bill and slowly swallowed it—headfirst!

This bird that preys so fearlessly upon poisonous snakes is the roadrunner. The body of the roadrunner is about 1 foot (30 centimeters) long. The bird has a slim, straight tail that is just about as long as its body. Roadrunners are found in the deserts and other dry parts of southwestern North America. They got their name because they are often seen running along roads.

Snakes are just one of the many kinds of creatures that roadrunners eat. Mostly, they eat centipedes, grasshoppers, scorpions, and spiders, including tarantulas. Roadrunners also eat lizards, toads, mice, smaller birds, and snails, as well as cactus fruits and some seeds.

A roadrunner kills a snake by stabbing the snake's head with its bill, lifting the snake up, and then hammering the victim on the ground. It kills most other creatures in a similar way. It holds the animal in its bill and pounds the head of the *prey* (animal hunted for food) against a handy rock or other hard object.

Most of the creatures a roadrunner hunts can move quite quickly. The bird has to be fast to catch them—and it is. A roadrunner can run at an average speed of 15 miles (24 kilometers) an hour. That's almost as fast as a sprinting human can run.

Roadrunners can turn, twist, and change direction in an instant. They can easily follow any prey that is trying to dodge away. And they are cunning—roadrunners sometimes lie in wait at drinking places and seize other birds that fly down for a drink.

Of course, a roadrunner does not really run all the time. Often, it just walks at a fairly fast pace. And, roadrunners cannot fly very well, so they take to the air only if they are frightened or are being chased. Even then, these birds never get more than about 10 feet (3 meters) off the ground for brief periods.

After a pair of roadrunners mate, the female does most of the nest building. She weaves twigs that the male brings her into a sort of shallow basket in a

cactus, bush, or small tree. She then lines this basket with grass, leaves, or other soft material.

The female lays from three to six eggs in the nest. She lays one egg every other day. Because *incubation* (keeping eggs warm so that they can hatch) begins with the first egg laid, some eggs hatch before others. A roadrunner nest often contains a few unhatched eggs, some small, weak, baby roadrunners, and an older, stronger youngster beginning to grow feathers.

Adult roadrunners feed their young the same things that they eat. Newly hatched roadrunners eat mostly insects. Older *nestlings* (growing birds still in the nest) are often fed lizards, which the parents stuff headfirst down the youngsters' throats. Sometimes, the lizard may be bigger than the young bird. The long tail of the reptile will hang out of the nestling's mouth for hours until the bird can swallow the rest of its huge meal.

Flying Sponges

Most of the Namib Desert of southern Africa is extremely dry. Only along the edges are there a few small, shallow ponds.

Some kinds of desert birds eat insects and other small animals that have a lot of water in their bodies. But sandgrouse eat mainly seeds and berries, so they still need to find water to drink. Once or twice a day, these birds may fly nearly 40 miles (65 kilometers) to get to a pond. After making sure that all is safe, the sandgrouse plunge their bills into the pond and drink.

Sandgrouse at a watering hole in the Kalahari Desert of South Africa.

When they are finished drinking, the male birds wade deeper into the water. They soak their breast feathers, which hold water like a sponge. Then each male flies to the nest where his three or four nestlings are waiting. He stands with his chest puffed out. The nestlings nibble and suck at his feathers and drink the water he has brought all the way across the desert.

Desert Homebuilder

In some of the deserts of southwestern North America, the gila *(HEE luh)* woodpecker serves as a sort of homebuilder for other desert creatures. In the fall, a gila woodpecker bores a hole into a giant cactus plant. The following spring, his mate lays her eggs in the hole. Their young hatch and grow up inside the hole.

The gila woodpeckers may reuse the nest site for several years before moving to a new location to raise their young. But the old nest does not stay empty for long! Cactus wrens, purple martins, owls, and other birds move into such abandoned woodpecker nests. Snakes, lizards, and sometimes even desert rats and mice may also move into the nests.

A gila woodpecker perches on a cactus in the Sonoran Desert in Arizona.

A great many desert creatures owe their homes to these tough, desert homebuilders that carve out a place to raise their family and then leave it for others when they move on. ✒

The Gibberbird

Some parts of Australia are covered with millions of small, round, smooth stones. The stones are known as *gibbers (JIHB uhrz)*, and the areas of land are called *gibber plains.*

A gibber plain is just about the most bare and desolate kind of desert there is. The plain receives very little rainfall, and it gets sizzling hot in summer. Still, a small bird called a gibberbird, sometimes called the gibber chat, makes this hot, dry, stony desert its home.

Why would a bird live in such a place? Mainly because there is plenty of food there for the bird. A gibber plain swarms with insects that love such hot, dry places. The gibberbird runs around over the stones, snapping up the insects as it goes. The bird hardly ever flies.

There are also plenty of seeds for a gibberbird to
find and eat. Although it seldom rains on a gibber
plain, whenever it does, millions of plants sprout from
seeds lying among the stones. The plants grow quickly
in the bright, hot sunshine. They soon die, but first
they produce billions of seeds. These seeds make new
plants after the next rainfall. The gibberbird gets what
water it needs from the seeds and insects it eats.

On the hottest days of summer, a gibberbird finds
the coolest, shadiest place it can, such as a hole dug by
a lizard. There, the bird stays, hardly moving. In this
way, it *conserves* (saves up) the energy and water in
its body.

All this may seem like a hard life, but gibberbirds
seem perfectly content to live as they do. The gibber
plain is their home, and they never leave it.

A Desert Elf

It is dusk on a desert in the American Southwest.
A giant cactus stands outlined against the setting sun.
High up on the side of the cactus, yellow eyes gleam
from a small hole. A tiny elf owl, the size of a sparrow,
stares into the gathering darkness.

During the day, the elf owl stays hidden in its cactus
home. Now, at dusk, it comes out and begins to call to
others of its kind. The yips and whistles of the little
owls resound through the desert. For such small
creatures, elf owls have very loud voices!

A beetle drones through the dusk and flies toward
the cactus. The owl shoots out of its hole. With one
clawed foot, the owl snatches the beetle out of the air!

Nighttime is hunting time for the elf owl. Like all
owls, the elf owl preys upon live animals. But because
it is so small, it must hunt small prey, such as flying
insects, which it grabs in midair. An elf owl will also
snatch up little creatures off the ground, including
crickets, grasshoppers, scorpions, and—on rare
occasions—small snakes and lizards.

Throughout the night, the little bird hunts. With the
approach of dawn, it heads back to its nest—a nest, in
this case, that it took over from a gila woodpecker. Elf
owls never make nests of their own. The elf owl pops
inside and settles down to rest during the long, hot day
that is about to begin.

*An elf owl looks out
of a cactus nest in the
Sabino Canyon of Arizona.*

Other Birds of the Desert

Black-tailed gnatcatcher

4 to 4 ½ inches

(10 to 11 centimeters)

Pink-breasted lark

6 inches

(15 centimeters)

Gambel's quail

10 to 11 ½ inches

(25 to 29 centimeters)

Cactus wren
7 to 8 ¾ inches
(18 to 22 centimeters)

Verdin
4 ½ inches
(11 centimeters)

Le Conte's thrasher
11 inches
(28 centimeters)

Birds

of the Sea and Shore

A Big-Mouthed Bird

It is probably true that a pelican's bill can hold more than its belly can. The underside of a pelican's lower bill is a piece of loose, rubbery skin. The skin stretches and swells to form a big pouch that can hold as much as 3 ½ gallons (13.3 liters) of water.

Many people think a pelican uses its big throat pouch for storing fish, but that is not true. A pelican's bill is a "scoop" for catching fish.

When a hungry pelican sees a fish swimming near the surface of the sea, the bird dives into the water and opens its mouth. Its pouch scoops up a large amount of

Photographs on pages 168—169

Pelicans and seagulls on the beach in Papudo, Chile, and an Inca tern.

water, as well as the fish. The bird shoots up to the surface and tips its head down to let all of the water drain out of its pouch. Then it lifts its head and swallows the fish.

Brown pelicans live along the coasts of southern North America, South America, and on nearby islands. They are big birds—about 4 feet (1.2 meters) in length. Stretched straight out, their wings can spread up to 7 ½ feet (2.3 meters). These birds look funny waddling about on land, but they are graceful gliders and fliers.

Brown pelicans like to live in groups. During the mating season, they may gather by the thousands. Where there are plenty of trees, the birds make their nests in treetops. Where there are few trees, they build their nests on the ground. Brown pelican nests are made of piles of twigs, leaves, grass, and dirt.

A mother pelican may lay from one to four eggs, but she usually lays three. At first, the baby pelicans are weak and helpless. Their eyes are closed and they have no feathers. But after a few days, they are strong enough to poke their heads into their parents' pouches for food. The parents squirt up bits of fish out of their stomachs for the baby pelicans to eat.

As the baby pelicans get older, feeding time is often wild and noisy—especially among pelicans that were born in nests on the ground. When they leave their nests, the young birds form large "gangs." When a grown-up pelican appears, all the young ones come

charging at it in the hope of getting food. Sometimes, the grown-up actually has to run away! But most of the time, it just pushes through the noisy crowd until it finds its own young and feeds them.

For a long time, brown pelicans were in danger of becoming *extinct.* (A species, or kind, of animal becomes extinct when every one of its kind has died.) Scientists feared that pollution might kill all of them.

Today, brown pelicans are doing better because of many years of scientists' efforts to protect these birds.

There are other kinds of pelicans, some of which are not sea birds. They may live near rivers and freshwater lakes in Africa, Europe, and Australia. Many of these birds catch fish by poking their heads underwater while swimming—not by diving. Otherwise, the ways of life of all pelicans are very much alike.

Whale Birds

Have you ever heard of a "whale bird"? It's not a bird that is as big as a whale, of course! It's a bird that got its nickname because it follows whales. Its real name is the red phalarope *(FAL uh rohp)*, although it's called the gray phalarope in Europe. The phalarope will fly above a whale, or even come down to *perch* (sit) on the whale's back.

As they *migrate* (move to a different area to find more food or a different climate), red phalaropes follow whales because the huge animals stir up many small sea creatures. These creatures come to the surface of the water, where the phalaropes can catch them easily. The phalaropes sometimes land on a

whale's back to search for small creatures that fasten themselves to the whale's body.

Red phalaropes live above or on the water most of their lives. They spend all winter at sea in warm parts of the world. During the winter months, their feathers are gray and white.

For about a month during the summer each year, the phalaropes become land birds. They migrate to the *tundra* (great icy plains) of the Far North. During this time, their feathers are mostly rust-colored and brown. While the tundra blooms with plants and buzzes with insects, the phalaropes mate, lay eggs, and raise their young. But they do this in ways that are different from most birds.

Instead of the male trying to attract a female, it is usually the female phalarope that tries to attract the male. And when the bigger and more brightly colored female has picked out a male she wants, she will not take no for an answer! She will bully him by pushing and pecking him until he simply gives up. Then she will threaten any female that comes near her mate.

It is the male who makes the nest. He pushes his body into damp, soft ground, and makes a shallow pit that he lines with grass and moss. The female lays three or four eggs in the nest. The male phalarope *incubates* the eggs (keeps them warm so they can hatch) and does all the work of raising the young after they hatch.

Sky Pirate!

A hungry gull gliding above the ocean spied movement in the water. Swooping down, the bird jabbed its bill into the water and caught a small fish. With the fish dangling in its bill, the gull soared upward.

But the gull did not know that it was being followed by a pirate. The pirate was a large, black bird with very long wings and an orange throat. And now it attacked! It darted at the gull, bumped the smaller bird and jabbed it with its bill. The frightened gull dropped its fish.

This was just what the pirate wanted. It dived after the fish, caught it in the air, and swallowed it. The poor gull flew off to look for another meal.

This pirate of the sky is the frigatebird, also called the man-of-war bird. A frigate *(FRIHG iht)*, also called a man-of-war, was a fast warship from long ago that was sometimes used by pirates. The bird got its name because it can be such a swift, bold robber. Most of the time, however, frigatebirds catch their meals without stealing them.

Frigatebirds live along seacoasts in warm parts of the world. Although they are faster and more powerful fliers than any other sea bird, they usually do not fly very far out to sea. They stay near land and snatch up fish and other sea creatures swimming near the surface—sometimes robbing gulls and other birds of the fish they have caught.

Male frigatebirds have an orange throat. At mating time, a male's throat swells up until it looks like a bright red balloon. This helps the male attract a mate.

The frigatebird's nest is a platform of sticks in a tree or on a rock or high cliff. Many frigatebird nests are near each other in *colonies* (groups of animals or plants of the same kind that live or grow in one place). A female frigatebird lays only one egg. Both she and her mate feed and take care of the young frigatebird. They must guard it well because other frigatebirds will eat it if given the chance.

Male frigatebird with throat sac inflated during a courtship display.

There Once Was a Puffin

From *There Once Was a Puffin*
by Florence Page Jaques

Oh, there once was a Puffin
Just the shape of a muffin,
And he lived on an island
In the bright blue sea!

Puffins spend a few months of each year living on
islands. The rest of the year, they live in the northern
seas, far from land. Fine swimmers, puffins use their
wings to move through the water. They also can fly,
but they spend much more time in the water than the
air. Puffins eat small fish and other tiny sea creatures
that they catch by diving and swimming underwater.

Puffins move to islands only at mating time. Using
their bills and feet, a mated pair of puffins digs a *burrow*
(hole) in which the female lays one egg. The male and
female share the job of incubating the egg. After the
egg hatches, both parents feed fish to the young puffin.

When the young puffin is almost ready to leave the
nest, its parents may visit it less often to feed it. The
young bird is big and can live partly off its fat while it
grows flight feathers. When the puffin is about 6 weeks
old, it leaves the nest and flutters down to the sea. It is
now completely independent from its parents, and it
learns to swim, fly, and catch fish all on its own.

People used to wonder how puffins catch fish.
A puffin often comes out of the water with several slim

fish hanging out of its bill. The fish must have been caught one at a time. But how does a puffin hold on to one fish when it opens its bill to catch another? Scientists have discovered that a puffin uses its tongue to hold the fish against its *palate* (the roof of the mouth) while it opens its bill to catch more fish.

A puffin can catch one fish after another without dropping any.

Sea Gulls

There is no such thing as a "sea gull." That's just the name most people use for almost any kind of gull — herring gulls, mew gulls, laughing gulls, ivory gulls, and others.

Most gulls are really shore birds, not sea birds. They rarely fly far out to sea. Instead, they gather on land in large groups called *flocks*. (A flock is a group of animals of one type that feed, live, or travel together.)

At mating time, gulls gather together in groups of thousands. Mated pairs fight for the nesting spots they want. Then the females lay eggs. The males group

together to guard their eggs from eagles—as well as
from other gulls, who might eat the eggs. After the
eggs hatch, mother and father gulls protect their young
for about six weeks, until they can care for themselves.

Gulls hunt, scavenge, and steal food on both water
and land. They will eat almost anything, living or dead.
Many gulls hang around ships and boats to feed on the
scraps thrown overboard. A laughing gull will even
stand on a pelican's head and snatch a fish right out
of its bill!

Gulls seem greedy—but their greed comes in handy.
Gulls help keep beaches clean, and they help farmers'
fields stay free of pests. In fact, gulls often follow farm
machinery and eat insects exposed by crop harvesting.

Shell-Opener

Have you ever seen someone trying to open an oyster shell? It's not easy to do, unless you have a special tool. And that is just what a bird called an oystercatcher has—its bill is a tool for opening oyster shells.

Oystercatchers live on sandy and rocky beaches in many parts of the world. The oysters and other shellfish they eat live on rocks in shallow water near the beach. When the tide goes out, the large clusters of shellfish are left uncovered. That's when flocks of oystercatchers show up for dinner.

When the oysters are uncovered, they open their shells just a tiny bit. An oystercatcher pokes its thin, pointed bill into the tiny crack. It snips the strong muscle that holds the two halves of the

shell together. Then, in an instant, the bird pries the shell apart and gobbles up the oyster.

Some kinds of oystercatchers use their bills to pry *limpets* and similar creatures off rocks. A limpet is an oysterlike animal, but it has only one shell that covers its back. It creeps over the rocks on its belly. A limpet can grip a rock so firmly that not even a strong person can pull the creature off. But the oystercatchers have flat bills that can slide between the limpet and the rock. The birds can then lift off the limpet, turn it over, and eat it.

Oystercatchers often wade in shallow water and pluck up snails and small crabs. The birds break open the shells by hammering them with their bills. They also sometimes push their long bills down into sand to catch worms.

Like many beach-dwelling birds, oystercatchers do not make much of a nest. The female just scrapes at the surface a few times. This makes a small hollow in which she lays her eggs. Although the eggs lie out in the open, they look so much like pebbles that it is almost impossible to find them.

Storm Birds

Sailors once believed that
when they saw the birds called
storm-petrels *(PEHT ruhlz)*, also
called stormy petrels, a storm was on
the way. And it is true that flocks of these
birds often gather around ships just before a
storm to shelter themselves.

There are actually 21 different kinds of storm-
petrels. They spend most of their lives far out over
the ocean, hundreds of miles (kilometers) from land.
When they need to rest, they just glide down to the
water, ride the waves, and float like corks.

Storm-petrels feed on tiny sea creatures that they pluck
from the water with their bills. When some kinds of storm-
petrels feed, they seem to be walking on the water with
their feet touching the sea's surface.

The only time storm-petrels come to land is
during the mating season. Some storm-
petrels make their nests under loose piles of
stones, while others dig tunnels with their
bills or use holes that they find. A mother
petrel lays one egg. She and her mate take
turns incubating the egg until it hatches.

Gooney Bird

European sailors once called it a "gooney bird." Today, Japanese fishermen call it an ahodori *(ah hoh DOH ree)*, or "fool-bird." The Dutch name for it means "stupid gull." But its real name is albatross *(AL buh traws)*.

On land or on the deck of a ship, the albatross looks silly. It waddles awkwardly and flaps its wings excitedly. And when it comes in for a landing, it often sprawls across the sand. But in the air, the albatross is graceful and beautiful. It can soar for hours without even flapping its wings.

Albatrosses are the largest of all sea birds. The wingspread of a wandering albatross can measure up to 11 ½ feet (3.5 meters). Albatrosses stay at sea for months at a time. They can even sleep while in the air! They feed on fish, squid, and scraps of food thrown from ships. The only time they come to land is to mate.

Wandering albatrosses come to land only once a year, to mate and raise a family.

Fish Hawk

The keen-eyed osprey *(AHS pree* or *AH spray)* soared in great circles along the coast. It peered down into the gray-green water as it flew. Suddenly, it dived and plunged its sharp-clawed feet into the sea. Moments later, it was back in the air with a large fish dangling from its claws.

Fish are slippery creatures that are hard to grasp and hang onto. But the *talons* (claws) of an osprey, also called a fish hawk, can grip with tremendous strength. And the bottom of each foot is covered with rough, spiky scales that act like little hooks. A fish simply cannot slip out of an osprey's clutches.

At mating time, ospreys build huge nests in trees, on top of telephone poles, or in other high places. The male brings fish to his mate. He gives her one piece at a time. She eats some pieces and tears others into smaller bits for her young, who wait quietly in the nest for their food.

An osprey clutches a fish with its talons.

Flying Through Water

You may think of penguins as fat, funny little birds who waddle about on ice and snow. And it is true that they waddle comically when they walk on land. But penguins are the finest swimmers of all birds. They swim and dive easily in search of small fish, squid, and the tiny crablike creatures they eat. In fact, they are swift and graceful in the water, and that is where they spend most of their lives.

The water is full of *predators* (animals that kill and eat other animals for food). Fast, sharp-toothed leopard seals and huge, swift killer whales search out penguins to eat. Nevertheless, the penguins go on land only to mate, lay eggs, and raise their young.

There are 18 different kinds of penguins, and they all live in the southern half of the world. At mating

Adult emperor penguins with their chick.

time, most kinds of penguins gather in groups of hundreds, or even thousands.

Emperor penguins gather in Antarctica in the fall. The female emperor penguin lays her egg on the Antarctic ice, and then she goes out to sea to feed. Her mate scoops the egg up onto the top of his feet. The egg is kept warm by a thick fold of skin that hangs down from his belly. The male penguin may stand for as long as two months keeping the egg warm. During all that time, he hardly moves and he never eats. Once the egg hatches, the father emperor penguin feeds the young penguin chick a nourishing, syrupy liquid from his throat.

Soon after, the mother penguin returns to the nesting ground. She calls out to the crowd in search of her mate. When her mate hears her call, he answers. Then the female emperor penguin makes her way to her family. She takes over raising the chick while the father goes out to sea and eats all the fish he can find.

Other kinds of penguins have different nesting habits. Adélie *(AD uh lee)* penguins also live in Antarctica, but they lay their eggs in the spring. They pile up stones to make their nests. Magellanic *(maj uh LAN ik)* penguins nest and raise their young in hollows in the ground or under bushes on the southern coast of South America. Little penguins, which are only 1 foot (30 centimeters) high, nest in burrows or under rocks on islands near Australia and New Zealand.

A Magellanic penguin incubating an egg. Unlike emperor penguins, both the male and the female Magellanic penguin incubate the eggs.

Other **Birds** of the Sea and Shore

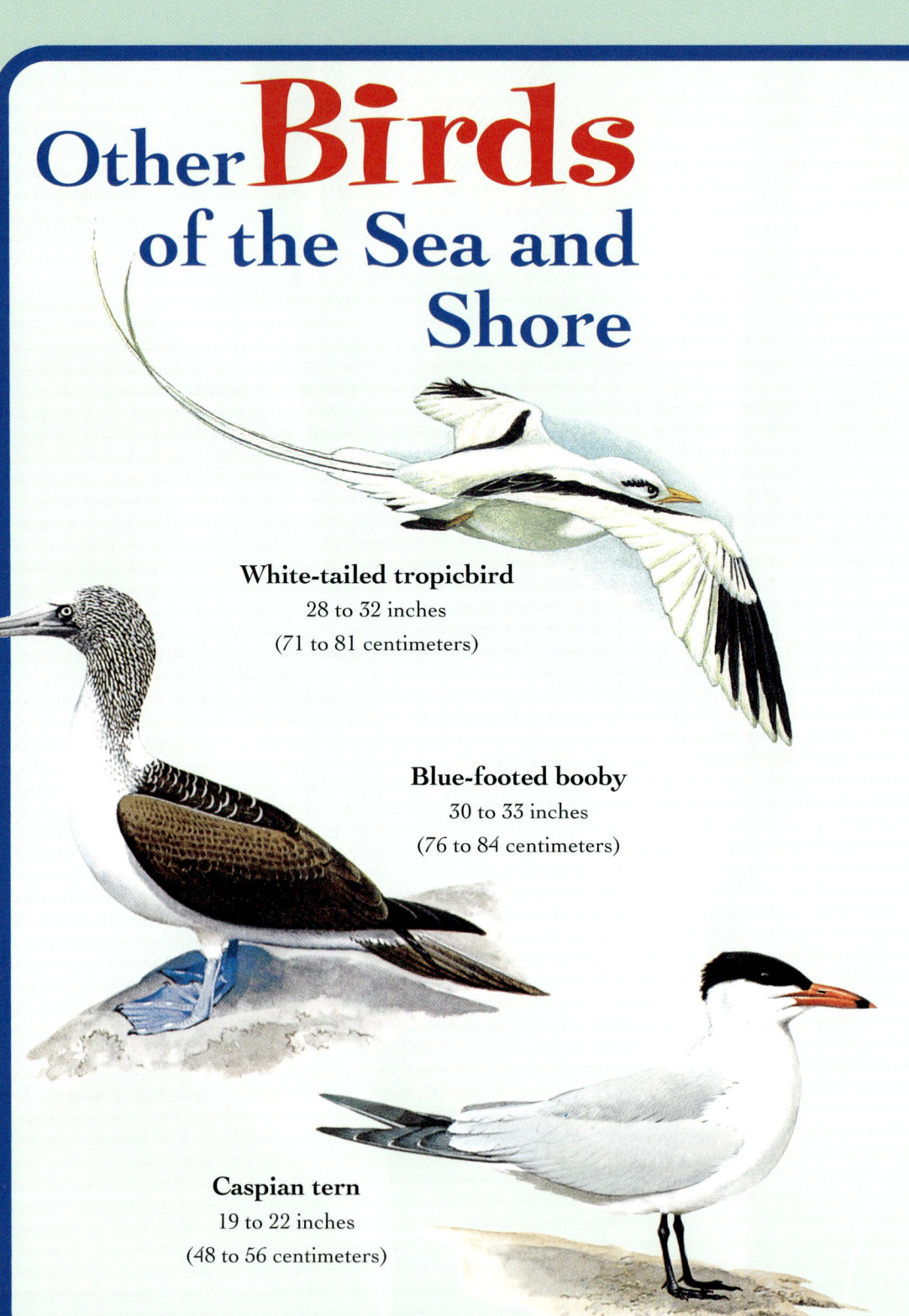

White-tailed tropicbird
28 to 32 inches
(71 to 81 centimeters)

Blue-footed booby
30 to 33 inches
(76 to 84 centimeters)

Caspian tern
19 to 22 inches
(48 to 56 centimeters)

South polar skua
20 to 22 inches
(51 to 56 centimeters)

Common tern
13 to 16 inches
(33 to 41 centimeters)

Wilson's plover
7 to 8 inches
(18 to 20 centimeters)

Double-crested cormorant
29 to 35 inches
(74 to 89 centimeters)

Black skimmer
16 to 20 inches
(41 to 51 centimeters)

Birds
of the
Far North

At Home on the Tundra

Spring has come to the *tundra*—that vast, icy plain that lies in the Far North. The ice covering the soil melts, giving seeds a chance to sprout. Grass and flowers shoot up. The alder, birch, and willow trees—no bigger than bushes—are shaggy with new leaves.

In a clump of grass, a bird crouches motionless. It is a bird with black, brown, and white feathers—a female willow ptarmigan *(TAHR muh guhn)*—sitting on her eggs. Her nest is just a little hollow that she scraped out of the dirt and lined with grass, leaves, and moss.

A shadow slides over the ptarmigan's body. It is a gull circling overhead. The gull drops lower, eyeing the bird on her nest. If the gull can frighten her into leaving, it can steal an egg or two to eat.

Photographs on pages 192—193

A pair of snowgeese and a young gyrfalcon.

The ptarmigan sees the gull and senses what it is up to. But she does not move. She merely makes a barking sound—a signal!

At once, a reddish-brown and white body shoots up from an alder tree not far away. It is the female's mate. He flies straight for the gull and smashes into it, knocking it to the ground. Then he sails back to his hiding place to continue his careful watch over his family.

The male willow ptarmigan is a fighter. He will fight fiercely to protect his mate and her eggs. In fact, he must be able to fight to get a mate.

In early spring, a male ptarmigan picks out a *territory* (an area an animal has chosen to live). He struts about, making cackling sounds—*karr-ack-ack-ack*! If another male appears, the owner of the territory cackles a loud war cry that sounds like, "go back, go back!" There is usually a fight that ends when one bird runs away. Only the strongest males can keep a territory and win a mate.

After baby ptarmigans hatch, both parents care for them and defend them until they can fly. During spring and summer, ptarmigans wander about, feasting on insects, seeds, and leaves. Toward the end of summer, there are many berries for them to eat. But spring and summer last for only a month on the tundra. Then, the temperature falls below freezing for the rest of the year, and life becomes more difficult.

Many birds and other creatures leave the tundra before this happens, but not willow ptarmigans. Most of these birds move only a short distance between their summer and winter homes. They are really fitted for life in harsh conditions.

Walking in snow day after day is impossible for most birds. Their feet would freeze. But short feathers on the willow ptarmigan's feet keep the feet warm. The feathers also act like snowshoes. They make it possible for the bird to walk on the snow without sinking in.

For most birds, living in a treeless, snow-covered land would be terribly dangerous. Hungry enemies would easily see the colors of the birds. Ptarmigans,

however, become snow-white in winter, except for a bit of the tail. This coloration makes the ptarmigans almost invisible against the snow, so that such enemies as arctic foxes or snowy owls have trouble seeing them.

Living on a flat, snow-covered plain with no place to *roost* (rest) is no problem for a ptarmigan. When one of these birds wants to sleep, it just digs into the snow. The bird's own body heat keeps this little "igloo" warm. For food during winter, a ptarmigan lives on the buds and twigs of the small alder, birch, and willow trees.

Willow ptarmigans are true citizens of the Far North. They are tough, hardy birds, well able to survive in a cold, snowy world.

A willow ptarmigan's feet are covered with feathers. This keeps the ptarmigan's feet warm and also helps the bird to walk more easily on snow.

Life of Danger

Snowy owls live in the frozen north. They mate in spring when the tundra blooms. But even in spring, life is far from easy. If the father owl cannot bring his young enough food, some of them will starve. Other owl young may become *prey* (an animal that is caught and eaten by another animal) for hungry foxes or gulls. When the snow is deep and an icy rain falls and freezes, the ground is covered such that the owls cannot get through the cover to catch their prey.

Snowy owls are *adaptable* birds. This means they can change their behavior to match changing conditions. They usually hunt for mouselike creatures called

A snowy owl with her chicks.

lemmings—but they also eat ptarmigans, rabbits, and other animals. Snowy owls usually hunt during the day. In the summer, when the sun does not set for weeks, their keen eyesight helps them find food. In the winter, when the sun does not rise, they rely more on their sense of smell. If they cannot find enough food, they head south, where bird watchers in the United States and other countries may be able to catch a glimpse of these beautiful birds at work.

Odin's Messengers

Long ago, in Scandinavia, people used to say that ravens were the messengers of Odin, the greatest of the Norse gods. Odin chose well, because ravens are very smart birds. They may team up to get food away from larger animals. Ravens sometimes play a type of game with sticks and stones, which they pass back and forth. They can even do acrobatics in the air.

Ravens are the largest members of the crow family. They live on mountains, plains, and deserts all over the northern half of the world. Many live on the tundra the entire year.

Ravens usually live in pairs. They take good care of their young. A mother raven prepares "baby food" for her young. First, she removes all the hard parts from the food. Then she fills her mouth and throat with water and food and mixes them together until the food is soft enough to give to her young.

Ravens will eat almost anything. They steal the eggs and young of other birds, feast on people's garbage, and eat the flesh of dead animals.

A common raven in flight.

Ruler of the Northern Sky

Streaking over the tundra, close to the ground, a gyrfalcon *(JUR fawl kuhn)* skims up and over a small rise. It crashes into a startled ptarmigan, killing it and then gobbling it up. The ptarmigan barely knew what hit it.

Gyrfalcons live on the tundra the whole year. They hunt mostly ptarmigans during the breeding season. In late spring and summer, they also hunt many other kinds of birds and small mammals. All falcons are good hunters. In the Middle Ages, people raised them to be hunting companions. Gyrfalcons were so prized that only kings were allowed to own them.

In the wild, gyrfalcons usually nest on cliffs near coastlines, where they take over the older nests of other birds. Young gyrfalcons hatch from their eggs when other types of birds are only beginning to lay eggs. So they are already skilled hunters when other birds are only beginning to learn to fly.

Snow Birds

Snow buntings spend the summer in rocky parts of the Arctic. Like many birds, they fly south for the winter. But for snow buntings, the "south" is not far. It is still in the northern part of the world, where the ground is covered in snow. There, the snow buntings eat seeds gotten from grasses and weeds half buried in snow.

As soon as the snow melts a bit, the buntings gather in large groups called *flocks* and head back to their northern home. Males each choose a territory, and females then join them. The birds use moss, grass, feathers, and bits of animal fur to make a nest under rocks or in cracks in the ground.

When the baby birds hatch, their mothers and fathers feed them mosquitoes, moths, spiders, and other tiny creatures. By fall, the young snow buntings can fly with their parents back to the snowy "south." *A snow bunting.*

Other Birds
of the Far North

Parasitic jaeger
16 to 21 inches
(41 to 53 centimeters)

Canada goose
22 to 40 inches
(56 to 102 centimeters)

Goshawk
26 inches
(66 centimeters)

Arctic tern
14 to 17 inches
(36 to 43 centimeters)

Purple sandpiper
8 to 9 inches
(20 to 23 centimeters)

Ross's gull
11 ½ to 13 ½ inches
(29 to 34 centimeters)

Lesser golden plover
9 ½ to 11 inches
(24 to 28 centimeters)

Find Out More

For Ages 5-8

Beaks! by Sneed B. Collard (Charlesbridge, 2002)

This picture book with simple text describes the beaks of various birds and explains how birds use their beak to hunt, gather food, and eat.

Bird Calls by Frank Gallo (Innovative Kids, 2001)

In this book, you will push a button to hear the sound of the bird, pull a tab to see a picture of the bird, and lift a flap to learn about it.

Birds by Stephen Savage (Raintree, 2000)

In this book, from the "What's the Difference?" series, readers will learn how birds catch a meal, how they hatch and raise chicks, and how flightless birds are able to get around.

Birds in Your Backyard by Barbara Herkert (Dawn Publications, 2001)

This picture book will help young naturalists develop an appreciation for the birds that may be found in their backyards. Specific information is given for common backyard birds that live in various regions of North America.

Feathers: Poems About Birds by Eileen Spinelli (Henry Holt, 2004)

This beautifully illustrated book is a collection of poems about different birds. At the back of the book, you will find fascinating facts about the birds represented in the poems.

Yahooligans! Animals: Birds
http://yahooligans.yahoo.com/content/animals/birds

On this Web site, users can click on a bird species and be linked to information about its habitat, size, description, location, and more.

For Ages 9 and Up

Birds (World Book, 2005)

This well-illustrated book from the "World Book's Science & Nature Guides" series is packed with information about birds from many different habitats. At the back of the book is a reference section that includes organizations devoted to birds and a glossary.

Birds of North America West by Jo S. Kittinger (DK Publishing, 2001)

Each page of this book from the "Smithsonian Kids' Field Guide" series focuses on one of the 140 birds included. Learn where the bird lives in western North America, where it makes its home, what it is commonly called, what it eats, and its size.

Looking for Seabirds: Journal from an Alaskan Voyage by Sophie Webb (Houghton Mifflin Co., 2004)

This illustrated book is a journal of the author's six-week research voyage studying sea birds on Alaska's Aleutian Islands chain.

100 Things You Should Know About Birds by Jinny Johnson (Mason Crest Publishers, Inc., 2003)

Fascinating facts from size to habitat to feeding habits of various birds are included in this colorful book.

The Life of Birds
http://www.pbs.org/lifeofbirds/

An extension of the PBS program, "The Life of Birds," this Web site provides information on the brains of birds. It also covers bird evolution, song, and parenting traits of birds.

Nature Songs
http://www.naturesongs.com

On this Web site, you can listen to the sounds of birds of North America and Costa Rica—not just bird calls or bird songs, but all the sounds birds make, such as wing sounds and bill rattles.

Glossary

alight *(uh LYT)* To fly down and land.

altricial *(al TRIHSH uhl)* Having to do with kinds of birds that are unable to see and usually have no feathers when they hatch.

binoculars *(buh NOK yuh luhrz)* Two small telescopes attached side by side so that a person can use both eyes at the same time to look at things that are far away.

brood *(brood)* To keep a baby bird warm and safe. A bird broods its young by crouching over them and protecting them with its wings.

burrow *(BUR oh)* A hole that an animal digs for a home or a hiding place. Also, to dig.

camouflage *(KAM uh flahzh)* To hide something by making it look like the things around it. Many birds have coloring and markings that help camouflage them.

colony *(KAHL uh nee)* Many animals or plants, all of the same kind, that live or grow in one place.

down *(down)* Fine, soft feathers.

endangered *(ehn DAYN juhrd)* For a *species* (kind) of animal or plant to be at risk of becoming extinct (dying without any survivors).

extinct *(ehk STIHNGKT)* A *species* (kind) of animal or plant becomes extinct when every one of its kind has died.

flock *(flok)* A group of animals of one type that feed, live, or travel together.

habitat *(HAB uh tat)* The place or area where an animal naturally lives and grows.

incubate *(IHN kyuh bayt)* To keep eggs warm so they can hatch.

instinct *(IHN stihngkt)* A natural way of doing something, without being taught how to do it. Birds build nests by instinct, without learning from other birds.

migrate *(MY grayt)* To move from one living place to another. Some kinds of birds, insects, and other animals migrate.

migration *(my GRAY shuhn)* The trip that animals make when they migrate, or change homes.

molt *(mohlt)* To shed old feathers, skin, hair, shell, antlers, or other things that grow on the body in order to make room for new growth.

nestling *(NEHST lihng)* A bird too young to leave the nest.

ornithologist *(or nih THOL uh juhst)* A scientist who studies birds.

perch *(purch)* A branch, wire, or similar thing above the ground on which a bird can sit and rest, or for a bird to sit or rest on such an item.

pesticide *(PEHS tuh syd)* A substance used to kill insects or other pests that damage plants, carry disease, or cause other problems.

plumage *(PLOO mihj)* The feathers of a bird.

precocial *(prih KOH shuhl)* Having to do with birds whose chicks have feathers and are able to see and run about when they are hatched.

predator *(PREHD uh tuhr)* An animal that kills other animals and eats them for food.

prey *(pray)* An animal that is caught and eaten by another animal.

roost *(roost)* To perch somewhere, to rest, or to sleep.

soar *(sawr)* To fly with the help of the wind or rising air.

species *(SPEE sheez)* A group of animals that share certain traits and are able to breed.

talon *(TAL uhn)* A large, curved claw.

territory *(TEHR uh tawr ee)* The area an animal chooses for a place to live.

threatened *(THREHT uhnd)* Having a chance of becoming endangered or extinct.

yolk *(yok)* The yellow part of an egg. In a bird egg, the yolk is food for the growing bird.

Index

This index is an alphabetical list of important topics covered in this book. It will help you find information given in both words and pictures. If there is information in both words and pictures, you will see the words *with pictures* in parentheses after the page number. If there is only a picture, you will see the word *picture* in parentheses after the page number.